REMEMBER THE ALAMO!

by
JEFF JEFFRIES

THE CHILDREN'S PRESS
LONDON AND GLASGOW

(Previously published under the title of
Davy Crockett, Frontiersman)

PRINTED AND MADE IN GREAT BRITAIN

CONTENTS

CHAPTER I

The Backwoods

THE LITTLE log cabin lay snugly in a clearing, won by months of back-breaking work from the virgin forest. Below the cabin the valley spread out, and through gaps in the trees the waters of the Nolachucky river glinted in the midsummer sun.

A settler, stripped to the waist, hacked steadily at the rampant weeds that threatened to engulf his crops. His son worked by his side, his muscles rippling rhythmically as he swung a hoe. Beyond the square of golden corn on the far side of the clearing, the younger children could be heard as they played hide-and-seek among the wild grape vines, and from the open door of the cabin came the sound of cooking pots rattling on the stove top.

The settler paused for a moment to wipe the perspiration from his forehead with the back of his hand. He stood leaning on his hoe and surveyed the clearing.

"Reckon we can be proud o' what we've achieved since we left Virginia, son," he said contentedly. "Never did think to see a crop o' corn growin' where those syca-mores were last fall."

They fell to discussing crops, forming plans for next

season, glad of a rest from the labours that started at sun-up and would go on until the light began to fade.

Neither of them noticed the parting of the fern fronds above them, nor did they see the swaying of the tall grasses on the edge of the clearing. They heard the call of a wild turkey and the answering call of its mate, but they paid no heed, for the wilderness all around teemed with game of every kind.

They never saw the naked, red-daubed Cherokees who slid through the undergrowth on their bellies, silently as snakes.

They died where they stood, clutching vainly at the flint-tipped arrows that pierced their breasts as the war-crazed Indians sprang into the clearing, screaming death to the white man.

Within minutes the whole family perished, the cabin burned, and the yellow corn lay trampled on the rich dark soil.

*   *   *

This was the world into which Davy Crockett was born, that hot August of 1786, in a similar cabin farther up the Nolachucky. It was a world of hardship, poverty and ever-present danger. Death stalked the forest glades and swampy valley bottoms; it lurked among the mountain crags, or in the thickets and cane-brakes of the lower levels—death from Indian tomahawk and arrow, or the steel-clawed pads of grizzly bear and mountain cat.

As the hunters and trappers fought their way over the Blue Ridge from Carolina and Virginia, hacking a path through the wilderness or striking off down salt-lick trails formed by generations of wild animals, the Creek and Cherokee Indians retreated westwards from their native lands. Log-cabins sprang up throughout the country that was to be the state of Tennessee, and the frontier moved steadily forward.

Close behind the trail blazers followed the settlers and homesteaders—poor farmers from the east who searched for new land on which to make a fresh start. They cut the forest trees to build their cabins, then burned the stumps and scrub to make way for the plough. They sowed corn, and ground the golden grain to make their bread. When they wanted meat to stock their larders or furs and hides for clothing, they took a rifle and hunted their quarry in the woods around.

Davy grew up in the woods. He learned the ways of the possum and the squirrel, the hiding places of the grinning coon, high in a gnarled tree, and the cheeky, darting movements of the chipmunk. He imitated their calls until he found them answering back. He stalked wild turkeys and gobbled at them in their own tongue. He tracked deer and yelled insults at the screeching parakeets that flew in flocks above the trees.

"That boy o' Crockett's grows more like an Indian every day," the settlers said as they watched him hunt, or saw him flash across the angry waters of the Nola-chucky in a flimsy, birch-bark canoe.

By the time he was sixteen, Davy's fame as a marksman had already spread beyond his home. He took on all comers at the shooting matches and found himself in great demand whenever a wolf hunt was arranged. "Get hold o' Crockett if you can," the word would go round before each hunt. "He can smell out a pack o' wolves five miles off, an' he don't reckon to waste a bullet in a whole day's shootin'."

As the years passed, Davy grew into a fine figure of a man. Six foot two in his deerskin moccasins, he loped noiselessly through the woods, his watchful eyes picking out the slightest sign of game. A crushed leaf, a hoof print in a bed of moss, a dropped feather or a claw mark on a twig—all had some meaning to the buckskin-clad hunter.

But as the farmlands pushed farther into the woods and scrub of the fertile valleys, the wild birds and game sought safer homes. Even the big, grey timber wolves found food hard to come by, and when the snows of winter approached they turned their attention to the hen roosts and the young calves and lambs of the settlers.

" It's no good, Polly," Davy said to his wife one day when he returned empty-handed from a long day's hunting. " There's too many settlers in the territory now. The game gets scarcer all the time. Another twelve months an' we'll forget the taste o' bear meat."

" But whatever shall we do for food this winter?"

Davy grinned. " Reckon we'll just have to starve," he answered, his eyes twinkling at her teasingly. " Unless . . ."

" Unless what? Davy Crockett if you don't tell me what you've been up to with that old Jake Marshall to-day I'll never speak to you again. I just know you've been planning something for days."

Davy smiled sheepishly. " Well, Polly," he said, " the fact is I've been thinkin' for a long time that I'd like my boys to grow up in new country where they can learn to hunt like I did. Let's go west, Polly, an' strike out fresh for ourselves."

" West?" Polly asked. " How far west?"

" Elk river. That's where we'll go. Jake hunted there last fall. Never seen so many bear in his life he said."

" Are there any Indians?" asked his wife, doubtfully.

" Indians? Sure. A few Cherokees, but they're all right now. It's those Creek varmints I can't abide. They'd scalp you as soon as look at you. Naked as the day they were born they are, an' smothered in red paint from tip to toe. Red Sticks they call 'em in those parts—but there ain't any there now."

" I hope not," said Polly Crockett.

CHAPTER II

One-Eye, the Cherokee

————— ⟨⟨⟨⟩⟩⟩ —————

"CRACK!" The sound of the shot welled up from the depth of the thicket, echoing back and forth among the rocks and crags of the terrain.

"Got you!" said Davy triumphantly as the smoke from the powder cleared. He saw the big, black bear stagger, stand motionless for a moment, then sink to the ground and lie still as a possum.

"Nice shooting!" exclaimed George Russell. "You drilled him clean through the head. There won't be a mark on that old bear's hide when we get him skinned."

"No sense in spoiling a fur for the sake of a little patience, George. A good hunter shoots to kill as clean as he can."

"I know," agreed Davy's neighbour. "There's too many men in the forest now who ain't got any idea o' huntin'. They blaze away regardless."

"Well that don't do for me," said Davy as he spun the ramrod down the barrel of his long rifle to remove the burnt powder and reloaded with the speed of long practice. He drew his hunting knife and picked his way through the undergrowth towards the ledge where the bear had fallen.

"Hold hard, George," he warned as the younger man pushed ahead, impatient to start the work of skinning while the light held. "Make sure brother bear is real dead before you go rushin' up on him like that."

"He's dead enough. He dropped like a lead weight."

"You never can tell." Davy kept a restraining hand on his friend's shoulder. They approached carefully, made sure the bear was in fact dead, and squatted beside the great carcass, studying the size and quality of the luxuriant fur.

"Shot a bear once, up towards the Blue Ridge," Davy went on reminiscently. "He lay as still as a log till I went to skin him. Then he woke up fast an' made a grab at me. If the dogs hadn't been with me I reckon that old bear would've skinned *me*."

"How was it he fooled you, Davy?" George asked. He could sit and listen to the famous bear-hunter's stories for hours on end.

"He didn't exactly fool me," Davy went on. "Fact was I fooled myself. The bullet only stunned him, an' he was mighty sore when I started to skin him alive!"

George chuckled. "I'll bet he was. What did you do?"

"Do?" echoed Davy, grinning broadly. "Man! What d'you think I did? Reckon I jumped nigh on forty feet in the air. I ran out o' that clearin' so fast I burned the soles off my moccasins!"

The two men bent to their work, Davy's razor-sharp knife slicing neatly down the underside of the bear, then out to each leg. George gripped the edges of the cut and started to peel the supple hide from the fat, warm flesh.

As they worked silently they heard a hail from the edge of the forest below.

" Well, bless my soul!" exclaimed Davy, rising to his feet. " I clean forgot about the boy."

He cupped his hands to his mouth and next minute the cry of a wounded panther screamed out from his lips, followed immediately by the death-rattle of a bull elk, the yelps of hunting dogs in full cry and the warning call of a turkey gobbler.

George Russell sat back on his haunches and roared with laughter. " That should fox the little fellow!" he spluttered as he regained his breath. " He'll think every crittur in the forest is after him."

" Not him," smiled Davy. " He knows the calls I make when I'm foolin'. Wait an' see what he does."

A moment later the neigh of a frightened horse was borne to them on the breeze, and as Davy's eldest son broke through the outer edge of the clearing, leading two pack horses, they heard a whole string of animal and bird calls issue forth. Father and son answered each other back with one call after another as the boy approached until it seemed to George Russell that the entire inhabitants of Noah's Ark were present on the mountainside.

" That must be a mighty big bear, Pa," said the boy as he struggled up the slope.

" How d'you know, son?" asked George. " You ain't seen him yet."

" Don't need to see a bear to tell how big he is. I measured his claw marks on a tree 'bout a mile back. Reckon he must've stood a good seven feet tall."

" Not so much o' your boastin'," Davy interrupted. " You give our neighbour here a hand to pack up those hams, while I get on with the rest o' the meat. We'll need to hang a deal of it up till to-morrow if we don't look lively."

An hour later the meat was expertly butchered, rolled in the deerskin pouches and strapped securely to the pack-saddle of one horse, while the other one took the carefully bundled skin on its broad back.

"How many bear does that make this season, Davy?" asked George Russell as they sat round the blazing log fire, relaxing after the long day, and enjoying the big meal of bear steaks that Polly Crockett had cooked for them.

Davy reached for the tally stick that rested in the corner of the cabin. It was covered in little notches, and he had a job to find space for recording that day's score.

"Hundred and five," he said at length. "That's since we moved to Bean Creek from Lincoln county last fall."

"Man alive! There ain't a hunter in the whole o' Tennessee can equal that tally. An' it don't take any account o' all the coon skins an' possum furs you trade down at Winchester settlement for goods and trinkets for Polly here."

"No George, I don't reckon to keep track o' every triflin' pelt I take an' cure," continued Davy modestly. "There's no tellin' how many deer I've shot besides. Nor yet how many other creatures fell to my rifle this year. I bagged four or five foxes last month, an' a panther an' two bob-cats the month before. It's been a good year—but the game's gettin' overdone like it is most places. I'm thinkin' o' movin' down Obion River way next fall."

"Here we go again!" exclaimed Polly, on hearing this. "I never knew such a man in my life, George. This husband of mine's got itching feet. He can't abide settling in one place longer than it takes to rear a brood of chicks. This is the third move we've made in five years as it is!"

George Russell laughed. "I believe you're as bad as he is, Polly. You get a kick out o' seeing new country an' makin' new friends. An' those boys o' yours certainly seem to thrive on it."

Next morning the two hunters were up early. They ate a hurried breakfast, and headed for the woods. There was a keen nip in the air to remind them that winter was not far away, and both men were glad of the three-quarter length coonskin coats that covered their hunting jackets. Davy pulled down the ear flaps of his fur hat and drew on mittens that left his fingers free for handling his rifle, while keeping his hands warm.

"Never did like the cold, George," he said, shouldering his pack and leading the way between the trees. "Sometimes I reckon I must have bear blood in my veins. When the first bite o' winter comes along I get the feelin' it'd be nice to hole up in a hollow tree until spring."

"Me too," agreed his companion. "Give me a good fire an' a tight little cabin, an' I won't poke my nose out o' doors all winter."

"But this is the time o' year I like best for huntin'," went on Davy as they forced their way through a cane-brake. "The new furs have grown on the wild creatures an' they've been eatin' so well to store up fat for the cold days ahead that they're fat an' lazy. I reckon to cut more notches on my tally stick this time o' the year than any other."

"What are we after to-day, Davy—bear again?"

"Just have to see what comes along, George. But I've

got a notion we may see somethin' o' the mate o' that bear we shot yesterday."

"Don't forget Polly wants possum meat for the stew pot, an' she told me she can do with a good fat wild goose as well. She needs the down for pillows."

Davy grunted. "I'll see what I can do about the possum," he said, "but I ain't shootin' any wild goose. Never did like killin' birds, exceptin' o' course a turkey-cock. The boy'll get the goose for her—he's gettin' pretty handy with a rifle now, but it'll be a long time before he can track a wild turkey. They're the most ornery, shy, cunnin', all-fired, difficult cusses to hunt that I know."

They pressed on through the belt of pine and firs that fringed the creek, jumping from stone to stone above the gurgling waters. They hadn't been travelling for more than half an hour when Davy found a possum lying in the undergrowth and looking for all the world like a fallen log as it shammed dead.

"We'll pick him up on the way home," he said as George helped him tie their first victim to a branch that projected high above the trail.

It was some hours later that they found sign of bear. Fresh claw marks showed in the bark of a huge old tree where the bear had climbed in its search for winter quarters. The two men pushed ahead, reading the spoor and moving noiselessly through the forest. Conversation died.

"Crack! Crack! Crack!" Three shots rang out suddenly to their left, about half a mile away, as near as they could judge.

"Looks as though we're not the only ones after Mr. Bear," said Davy, straightening up from examining the tracks.

"Better see if we can give 'em a hand," suggested George.

Presently they came to a ridge. They clambered up and looked about for a sign of the hunters. Davy saw them first.

"Cherokees," he muttered, briefly.

A hunting party of half a dozen braves were clustered round the bulky form of a bear they had recently hauled out from a nearby thicket. They jabbered and gesticulated to each other, unaware of the two white men who watched.

"Why, it's old One-Eye an' his sons from over on Silver Creek," Davy exclaimed as the aged Indian turned towards them. "Let's go and have a word with him."

At their approach, One-Eye stepped forward and raised his hand in welcome.

"Peace be with you, brother," he said.

"Greetings, O mighty hunter," Davy replied in the Cherokee tongue.

George Russell stood back and listened as Davy and the old Indian leaned on their rifles and chattered away to each other in the tongue-twisting language of the tribe, of which he understood but a few words. It was clear from the signs by which the two men conversed, that the Indian was describing the bear hunt in detail, from beginning to end, while Davy congratulated him upon his wisdom and skill. What puzzled George was the length of the conversation and the way in which it ended, with One-Eye pointing repeatedly to the south-east and shaking his head worriedly.

"What was all that about?" asked George as they made their way home.

"He was only telling me the story o' the hunt," Davy answered. "They always do. But he said something else that I don't like much."

"Was that when he kept pointing over the mountains?"

Davy nodded. "He said the woods were full of evil tales that spoke o' war smoke in the villages o' the Creeks."

"Oh, that's just Indian talk," George exclaimed scornfully. "They're always tryin' to throw a scare into us—it's their kind o' joke."

"I know all about that," Davy replied. "But I know old One-Eye. He's a good Indian an' if he says it's true, then I'll wager a silver dollar to a coonskin that the Creeks'll be on the warpath before the winter's out."

CHAPTER III

The War Drums Sound

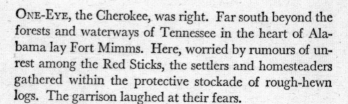

ONE-EYE, the Cherokee, was right. Far south beyond the forests and waterways of Tennessee in the heart of Alabama lay Fort Mimms. Here, worried by rumours of unrest among the Red Sticks, the settlers and homesteaders gathered within the protective stockade of rough-hewn logs. The garrison laughed at their fears.

"Don't you worry about a few Injuns," said the soldiers. "Wait an' see how the Red Sticks run when they feel the bite of an Army bullet."

Tecumseh, chief of the Creek nation, bided his time, gathering his warriors from valley and swamp, forest glade and river gully—and all the while the war smoke spoke back and forth from village to village.

Squaws sat cross-legged by their huts, mixing the paints and pigments with which to daub their menfolk; young braves sharpened their tomahawks or fitted new feathers to their arrows; the elders tested their bows and dreamt of the scalps that would hang on the totem pole before the full moon bathed the forests in its silvery light.

Day after day Tecumseh waited, making no move, and presently the settlers grew restive and began to drift back

to their farms to tend their stock. The soldiers swung
open the great wooden doors of the fort to let them pass.

And then Tecumseh struck.

From behind every boulder, tuft of grass and tree the
painted warriors sprang. Howling like jackals after a
wounded deer they poured in through the doors, slashing,
stabbing, lunging at the startled soldiers as they screamed
the war cries of their tribe.

From the hollows by the river and the woods all
around, an endless stream of Indians ran to the attack.
They carried huge logs of exactly the right size to block
the loopholes high in the stockade from which the white
men fired and fired again—scarcely pausing to aim at the
tight packed mass of Red Sticks. As fast as one Creek fell,
another took his place.

Within half an hour the battle was over. Attacked from
inside the fort and out, their loopholes blocked, the soldiers fell back to the garrison buildings with the settlers
they had boasted they would protect. Here they fell and
were scalped coldly, mercilessly, until not a single man,
woman or child remained alive within the fort.

Tecumseh leered triumphantly when his braves returned with details of their victory. " This is but the beginning, my warriors," he told them. " Pass word among
the villages of our people that they may rejoice. Take
tidings of this mighty battle even into the lands of the
Choctaws and of the Chickasaws. Let every one of our
brothers know Tecumseh has struck the first blow, and
soon the white dogs shall be driven from our country."

*   *   *

But Tecumseh underrated his enemies.

The news of the massacre sped through the forest, passing from mouth to mouth. Within days a dozen different tales were circulating through the backwoods of the frontier and far east among the big towns and ports of the coast. Exaggeration followed exaggeration, rumour followed rumour, until the facts of the Indian rising were barely recognisable. But details mattered little, for of one thing all were certain. The Creeks were on the warpath, and the sooner they were taught a lesson the better.

It was George Russell who brought the news to Davy Crockett. He burst into the clearing in front of the hunter's cabin, and reined his straining mount to a halt before the open door.

"Davy! Davy!" he yelled. "Old One-Eye was right."

The tall hunter stepped into the doorway and looked severely at his young friend. "Now what in creation's got into you?" he asked. "Hollerin' an' yellin' an' carryin' on as if you had a pack o' Indians on your tail."

George swung down from the saddle and twisted the reins around the hitching post. "That's about what I have got, Davy. We're in for trouble sure enough."

Davy Crockett frowned. "D'you mean to say the Creeks are on the warpath after all?" he asked.

George nodded. "That's about the measure of it. Tecumseh took Fort Mimms not six days ago. Not a single survivor to tell how it happened."

"Did he, by heaven!" Davy pushed his coonskin cap back from his forehead and scratched thoughtfully at his shock of jet-black hair. His face was grim, hard. His cool, grey eyes had lost their customary twinkle; they glinted, steel-like below his thick, dark brows. George Russell felt a shiver pass over him. He'd never seen his friend look like this before. Gone was the kindly, story-telling hunter; in his place had appeared a man he didn't recognise—a man he would hate to have for an enemy.

"Tell me all you know, George. But keep it short. Where did you hear this?"

"Down at the settlement. I was tradin' some furs in at the store when Luke Peters pulled into town. He's been workin' a trap-line up towards the Ridge. Says the woods were fair buzzin' with the news. A party o' Cherokees told him Tecumseh had a thousand braves in war-paint."

"Nonsense!" Davy spat scornfully at a hickory log. "He may have a thousand now, an' more, but I'll stake my life he didn't have more'n two-three hundred at the fort. Those Creeks are cunnin', they'd hang back to see what happened to Tecumseh an' his hot-heads afore they'd join him. Now they'll flock to him by the score."

"That's about the size of it," George agreed. "But what's to stop them sweepin' through here now they're really on the warpath?"

Davy looked up at his young friend. He studied him carefully before he answered, and he liked what he saw. George Russell was not above twenty-one, if that. But age meant nothing, for men matured early on the frontier. What Davy saw was a slim, wiry frontiersman, broad-shouldered, clear of eye and sure of himself. He read courage in the young man's eyes and in the line of his jaw. He smiled grimly and saw an answering smile spring into the other's eyes. He winked slowly, deliberately.

"What's to stop 'em, George?" He repeated the young man's question. "I'll tell you what. You an' me, an' a

few hundred more like us. We've got to slam that mur-
derin' heathen so hard he'll wish he'd never been born!
Are you with me?"

"When do we start?"

Davy grinned. "Right here an' now," he answered,
reaching for his rifle.

CHAPTER IV

Into Indian Territory

———————/⟨≋⟩/———————

"WELL, Major, what do you make of them?" asked the captain of militia.

Major Gibson pushed his uniform hat firmly into place at the correct angle, straightened his tunic and took a deep breath before answering. If he spoke his mind he was sure to offend the captain—and that would never do. General Jackson had told him most pointedly to use tact with the volunteers he was to command, and that meant with their officers as well.

"Don't forget, Gibson," the General had said before he left. "They're not soldiers—yet. They're hunters, trappers and settlers from the backwoods. They've got no respect for an Army officer or even an Army uniform. But they know the woods, they understand Indians, and if their dander's up they'll fight like wild cats. See what you can do with them."

"They're very—er—*impressive*," the major said at length. He was more than surprised when the captain burst out laughing.

"What you mean, Major, is that they're the rummest

bunch of rough necks you've ever seen in your life, isn't that so?"

Gibson chuckled. He was beginning to like this captain who only three days before had been a small-town lawyer. "As a matter of fact that's exactly what I *was* thinking," he agreed. "Quite frankly, if I were a Creek I'd be scared out of my life at the very sight of them! How many have you mustered?"

"Eight hundred."

"Have you by Jove! That'll please the General. But now I must pick some men for a scouting party. Can you recommend any man in particular to come with me and choose his companions?"

The captain didn't hesitate. "Crockett's the man for you, Major," he said at once. "Come and see what you think of him."

They passed out through the flap in the tent and made their way to the tavern where Davy was swapping tall hunting tales with Luke Peters, Jake Marshall and a dozen other old friends over a horn of ale.

"I'm game for anythin', Major," Davy drawled, studying the regular from under lowered lids. "I'll go with you, an' I'll take young George along with me for company."

"But he's only a boy!" protested Gibson. "Why, he hasn't a whisker on his face!"

"If it's whiskers you want, Major, we'd better take a goat along," came the drawled reply.

Gibson laughed. "You pick your men, Crockett, and I'll pick mine."

He looked around the room at the massed volunteers. They were of all shapes, sizes and conditions. Some wore suits of grey and blue homespun, others sported fringed leather coats and fur hats; yet others wore the garb of prosperous storekeepers, the smocks and leggings of wagoners or the jerseys and slouch hats of rivermen. All carried rifles, and all looked as though they knew how to use them.

Among the bearded faces he spotted one that stood out from the others like a prickly pear in a desert. Bright red whiskers sprang from the man's chin like the quills of a porcupine; cool, untroubled eyes stared back into his own as he stopped in front of the hunter.

"Looks as if I've found my goat," he said with a grin, and as the laughter greeted his choice he knew that he had been accepted by the men he was to lead.

Within half an hour the scouting party was chosen, their horses saddled, rations drawn and they were ready to move off. Gibson swung up into the saddle of his bay mare and led the way past Beaty's spring to the ford across the Tennessee River.

"We'll split forces a mile or two inland, Crockett. I'll strike off to the east with my herd of bearded goats, while you take your beardless boys to the west. We'll meet back at Ditto's Crossing in four days. Remember, we're after information—not scalps. If you strike a war party, break away and get back as fast as you can. Understand?"

Davy nodded. "Yes, sir," he said, the unaccustomed "sir" sounding oddly on his lips.

With muttered "good lucks" passing between the men, the two parties separated and disappeared into the woods. Davy led his six volunteers down a narrow, twisting deer track, forcing his way through the overhanging branches of hickory and birch that tried constantly to tangle with his tall form. Presently the track opened out into a narrow valley, and in the distance he saw the smoke from a fire.

"Shin up that tree, young George," he said, " an' tell me what you see."

George Russell sprang off his horse. He made short work of climbing a tall oak that commanded a view of the lower part of the valley.

"There's a cabin o' sorts," he called down. "Looks like a tradin' post. No one about."

"Good," said Davy. "Let's go an' have a look-see. We might pick up some news o' the Creeks from the trader."

They approached carefully, ringing the woods on either side of the clearing in which the cabin lay. They kept their eyes peeled for any fresh sign of Indians, but there were no tracks visible. Behind the cabin a half-breed Cherokee worked at a deer skin, fixing it securely to a drying rack for curing. He looked up in surprise as Davy rode out from the woods in front of him.

"No Red Sticks come this way," he told them in answer to their questions. "This Cherokee country. Ride south and have words with the braves at my mother's village."

"Can you show us the way?"

The half-breed shook his head. "No. Not while the sun is awake. But when the sun sleeps so will I come to the place where the roads meet and lead you to my village."

"Seems he was just about as scared of the Red Sticks findin' him workin' for us as I am o' meetin' any o' the varmints myself," said George as they remounted and rode off towards the creek that would lead them to the meeting place.

"You ain't the only one, son," muttered Jake Marshall, half to himself. "I've had prickly feelin's runnin' up and down my spine ever since we rode into the woods."

"Me too," came the voice of Luke Peters from behind.

Davy laughed. "Time enough to worry about Red Sticks when we get among 'em."

"Then it'll be too late," said Jake.

They were all glad when they broke out of the trees and into open country along the creek. They shook their horses into a steady lope and headed for the fork in the trail.

It was late afternoon when they struck the first sign of habitation—a small homestead consisting of a log and mud cabin, a good-sized hay barn and a few acres of indian corn. A small horse pasture in front was roughly fenced with split log rails. Davy drew rein to allow the others to come level then gestured them to spread out and approach at a walk.

They were strung out along the fence when a Creek squaw stepped through the door of the cabin. She took one look at them, turned and ran screaming back into the cabin.

"Don't make sense," said Davy, speaking out of the corner of his mouth to Jake. "Never knew an Indian to farm like a white man."

"Nor me," grunted Jake, his eyes fixed on the doorway as his thick thumb bore hard on the hammer of his flintlock and snapped it to full cock.

Next moment the answer lay before them, for out of

the cabin stepped a burly white man, clad in the usual buckskin breeches and moccasins, but wearing Creek amulets and charms upon his bare arms and bull-like neck. Standing by his side were two young half-breeds.

" Great sufferin' snakes! A White Indian!" George Russell exclaimed, lowering his rifle.

CHAPTER V

The White Indian

———————⟨✦⟩———————

"WHAT DO you want here?"

The man's tone was surly. Davy took an instant dislike to him.

"We're scoutin' for General Jackson," he said. "Have you seen anything of Tecumseh's war party?"

The White Indian hesitated before answering. "I know nothing of Tecumseh," he said at length. "I am blood-brother to the chief of my wife's village—but they are peaceful Creeks, of a different tribe to Tecumseh. We want no trouble with the Army."

"So you've seen no sign of hostile Creeks through here?"

Again the man hesitated, and Davy was certain he knew more than he was saying. He raised his rifle and pointed it straight at the man's heart. "I'll give you thirty seconds. Talk—and talk fast—or by heaven I'll shoot you down like the skunk you are!"

"I want no trouble," the man protested, turning pale beneath his tan. "All I know is that we saw ten painted warriors pass through the woods at dawn. They didn't stop. Now go, before they return and take our scalps for helping you." He turned abruptly and walked back into the cabin, followed by his two sons.

Jake spat expressively. " There ain't nothin' worse than a white man who goes native," he said. " Let's get out o' here, Davy."

" We'll get out when we're good an' ready, Jake. I feel as though I could eat ten Creeks for supper, feathers and all. If there's a war party about, the Cherokees will know. I'm not goin' back till I've talked with the chief o' their village."

By nightfall they had reached the rendezvous, but there was no sign of the half-breed trader who was to guide them to the village. They found a wooded hollow on a slope that commanded a clear view of the two trails, and made camp.

Bright moonlight flooded through the trees as they un-saddled and tied their horses close to hand. They sat and waited in silence, chewing on the dry jerky and biscuits from their pouches, pausing every now and then to cock an ear to the noises of the night.

Davy sensed a tension among his companions that matched his own uncertainty. Somewhere in those woods below were ten Creeks who had sworn to kill every white man they came upon. They might be all around his party now, or they might be more than twenty miles away. There was no telling.

A stealthy rustle came suddenly from behind the hollow, making them all jump.

" What was that?" whispered one of the scouts in Davy's ear.

" Don't you know a chipmunk when you hear one?" asked the hunter scornfully. The rustle came again, and with it the soft chatter of the little animal as it prepared for sleep. Then, a second or two later, the hoot of an owl broke the stillness of the night, from lower down the track.

"Here comes our 'breed," said Davy, rising to his feet and hooting in reply. The call came again as the men gathered their kit, and made ready to saddle their horses. It was nearer this time, and as Davy replied with the hunting screech of a grey owl they saw the half-breed slip from the shadows and move towards the hollow.

The village of the half-breed's mother proved to be only a bare three miles away. As they stepped into the circle of cooking fires the chief rose and made them welcome.

"We have seen no Creek dogs," said the old man when Davy had told him of their mission. "If they had passed this way my braves would have come upon them as they hunted deer in the forest. But stay and take meat with us, white brothers, and rest your horses."

"Now that's what I call a real bright idea!" exclaimed George Russell, relaxing for the first time that night. "What d'you say, Luke?"

"Suits me," grunted the trapper, cheering up at last.

But they barely had time to swallow the first mouthful of deer meat which the squaws had prepared when a Cherokee brave ran into the clearing, shouting at the top of his voice.

Davy and Jake pushed their way through the braves who gathered around the man and tried to pick up what it was he was telling them.

"What's he say?" asked the other scouts, following close on their heels.

"Can't make it out," said Davy, frowning in concentration. "He talks too fast for me. Any luck Jake?"

"Somethin' about Creeks, but I can't fathom his lingo. He's chatterin' like a squirrel."

A minute or two later the chief stepped from the group of Cherokees and drew Davy on one side. His face was grave.

"You will have to go, white brother," he said. "This man tells of a big war party who have been crossing the southern river by the Ten Islands. If they come this way we shall all be put to death."

"How many warriors?" Davy asked.

The chief held up both his hands, his fingers spread wide. "Ten times ten times ten," he answered dramatically.

"Jumpin' cats! A thousand o' the critturs!" Davy swung round and rattled out a stream of orders. "George! get those horses saddled. Luke! grab enough o' that deer meat for all of us, an' pack it in a pouch. We'll have to eat as we ride."

"What's the hurry, Crockett?" The voice of one of the scouts broke in. "Ten Islands is far south o' here. We've got time to eat in comfort."

Davy turned upon the man. His eyes swept over him contemptuously. "Don't you ever think about anythin' but your stomach, Jim Masters? If we don't get back an' warn our boys the Creeks'll cut through between them an' the general's force at Fayetteville. There's not a moment to lose."

"Means ridin' all night," muttered Jake, grumbling as always. "Who'd be an Indian fighter! Wish I'd never left my little log-cabin."

Davy grinned at him. "The day you stop moanin', Jake, I'll know we're in real trouble. You won't be happy until you're in the thick of a good battle."

"Maybe you're right, Davy," said the old hunter, his face breaking into a rare smile. "It's like shootin' wild duck. When there's a whole flock o' them you can't help but knock a few down. But when the pesky critturs split up in twos an' threes they've come an' gone afore you're ready for 'em."

"Well, it looks as though a flock o' Red Sticks is on its way, an' coming fast."

"Let 'em come," said Jake, spurring out of the camp ahead of the others. "I'll sting their tail feathers for 'em!"

*　　　　*　　　　*

Back at Ditto's Crossing, Colonel Coffee, a hard-bitten old war-horse of a soldier, had arrived with a detachment of foot volunteers to take command of the entire force—of which Major Gibson's mounted scouts formed but a small part. Among the new arrivals were a party of Cherokees, and even a handful of Creeks who had no love for Tecumseh.

Frontier warfare did strange things, turning Indian against Indian and white man against his own kind, until the bewildered volunteers scarcely knew who was their enemy and who their friend.

It was to Colonel Coffee that Davy Crockett reported with news of Creeks massing among the shoals and islands of the Coosa River. Major Gibson had not yet returned from his sortie.

"D'you mean to stand there and tell me there's a *thousand* of them?" the colonel roared. "Why, that's more men than I've got in my whole command."

"That's what the Cherokee told us, Colonel. But we didn't see hair nor hide of a Red Stick while we were out."

"Then I don't believe it," said the colonel flatly. "We'll wait and see what Major Gibson has to say. Dismiss!"

Davy was fighting mad when he got back to his friends.

"Of all the stupid, ignorant, blunderin' old nanny-goats!" he exploded, "that blisterin' colonel takes the prize."

"Why, what's up, Davy?" asked the scouts, gathering round the black-haired hunter who stood head and shoulders above them, his eyes blazing with anger.

"What's wrong? I'll tell you what's wrong. We're just volunteers, who bring our own rifles, ride our own horses and wear our own clothes. We're nobody, accordin' to the colonel. He don't even believe us when we nearly break our necks gettin' back with a report. If we were regulars, all dressed in white pantaloons an' brass buttons an' soldierin' for the pay, he'd believe us. You wait an' see what happens when Gibson gets back with the same news. That old colonel will move like a streak of lightnin'."

Major Gibson's party returned three hours later. Saddle-weary, and red-eyed from lack of sleep, they splashed their lathered horses across the ford while Davy and his companions lay sleeping—their rifles ready primed and their horses saddled for instant action. The major's report was identical.

Within minutes the camp was buzzing like a beehive. Orders poured forth from Colonel Coffee's tent. A runner galloped down the trail to Fayetteville with urgent dispatches for General Jackson. Double guards were mounted. Scouts took up positions in the woods from which they could give early warning of an attack. Foot soldiers made the earth fly as they threw up breastworks round the camp.

"Drat the Army!" grumbled Jake Marshall, woken from a sound sleep by the ring of a shovel on rock close by his ear. "Don't even let a feller sleep when he's off duty."

"What's goin' on?" Davy came to with a start, grabbing instinctively for his rifle.

"Just your friend the colonel playin' at soldiers," said Jake, sourly. "There he goes. Tearin' round the camp like his pants were on fire!"

A slow smile spread over Davy's face as he caught sight of the colonel mounted on a big white stallion, coming to a halt by a group of soldiers who struggled to get a fallen tree into position on the defences. "Hurry, men! Hurry! Those red devils may be on us by nightfall." The words drifted back to Davy's ears and his smile widened into a grin.

"Looks like he's doin' a bit o' *believin'* for a change," he chuckled.

By sunset the rough trenches were dug and the soldiers lay shivering on the cold damp soil, huddling together for warmth. An uneasy peace descended upon the camp. Hour after hour ticked slowly by. Sentries and scouts were relieved and new ones posted. Men talked in hushed whispers as though their words could be overheard by the

unseen enemy, and the light of a tallow candle in Colonel
Coffee's tent proclaimed that the commanding officer was
passing a sleepless night.

Dawn came creeping slowly across the eastern sky; wild
birds trilled their morning greeting to the sun and small
animals woke in their nests and burrows. A flight of wild
duck winged its way above the tree-tops, watched hungrily by the unshaven sentries—and still the Red Sticks
kept away.

It was midday before General Andrew Jackson rode
into the camp at the head of the main army. Thirteen
hundred foot volunteers marched behind him, footsore
and hungry after their thirty-five mile forced march from
Fayetteville.

" Won't be long before we see some action now Old
Hickory Face is here," said Davy, watching the grey-
haired general dismount.

" He don't look too happy," grunted Jake.

" If you ask me, he's a sick man," said George Russell,
taking in the famous soldier's drawn face and sallow skin.
" One o' the men just told me he was wounded in a duel
a few months back."

" Sick or well, he's a fighter, son. I shouldn't like to
be in Tecumseh's shoes one little bit."

CHAPTER VI

The Elusive Enemy

GENERAL JACKSON wasted no time.

"I want to see the scout who first brought news of the Creeks to you, Colonel," he demanded. "Major Gibson tells me this man got back before he did. I need smart men. Send him straight in to me."

Davy was puzzled when the general's message reached him.

"Wonder what Old Hickory Face wants with me?"

"Goin' to give you a raise in pay, I reckon," said George.

"Shouldn't be surprised," agreed Jake. "But twice nothin' is still nothin', so he won't retire with a fortune!"

Davy reported at once and was shown in to the general's tent. Jackson got to the point immediately.

"I want you to become my chief scout, Crockett. How would you like that?"

Davy shook his head. "No, General," he said. "I shouldn't like it."

Jackson was amazed. "Why ever not?" he demanded.

The tall hunter looked his commander-in-chief straight

in the eyes. "Because it would mean mixin' with too many fool Colonels, Majors an' Captains," he drawled.

"And Generals?" Jackson asked, slyly.

Davy was unperturbed at the question. He shrugged his shoulders. "Maybe," he answered. "That remains to be seen, but from what I've heard, *you're* no fool. Fact is," he added with a grin, "they tell me you're as wily as a fox about to raid a hen roost!"

The General burst out laughing. "Let's hope they're right, Crockett. Anyway I'm not taking 'no' for an answer. You will be my chief scout. That's an order."

"It's your Army, General," said Davy, dryly. "Tell me what you want an' I'll see what I can do about it. But I'll have to work in my own way."

"That's what I like to hear, Crockett. I want information about these tarnation Red Sticks. Where are they now? How many are there? Why haven't they attacked yet? I want answers to all those questions and a dozen more besides. How you get the information is your business, but I want it; I want it fast, and I think you're the man to get it for me."

An interested gleam came into Davy's eyes. "Now you're talkin', General," he exclaimed. "I've been thinkin' about those Red Sticks. There's somethin' fishy goin' on, an' there's only one way to find out what it is."

"What's that?"

"Ride into their territory in force an' ferret 'em out like stirrin' bears out of a cane-brake. Take your foot soldiers down to the Coosa, while I guide a big force o' mounted volunteers round on the far side o' the river. One of us is bound to strike Tecumseh an' we'll be strong enough to thrash him wherever we find him."

"Sounds sense to me, Crockett. Be ready to move off at first light to-morrow."

*   *   *

Six hundred mounted scouts and rangers formed Davy's force. They back-tracked through Huntsville settlement, swung south and crossed the river at Melton's Bluff. Deep into Indian territory they thrust, looking for trouble, and riding fast to meet it.

Davy and a carefully selected band of men, superbly mounted on the best of the horses, spread out ahead of the main party, scouring the country for Tecumseh and his warriors. They took advantage of every ridge and hilltop from which to scan the terrain. They climbed trees to obtain a better view, and followed obscure trails that petered out at water holes—and everywhere they drew blank.

A thousand Red Sticks had disappeared into thin air— yet wherever the scouts penetrated they found recent tracks of moccasined feet, a broken arrow here, a goose feather there. At one point Davy came upon the freshly-killed carcass of a deer, still warm to the touch, but of the hunters there was no sign.

"Beats me," Davy admitted at length. "How in blazes can you fight an enemy you can't see?"

"They'll show up fast enough when they reckon we're tired out," said the pessimistic Jake. "Another few days an' the boys'll be too durned tired to fight. Food's gettin' mighty scarce already, an' no man can fight on an empty stomach."

"That's true," agreed Davy. "But I've got a feelin'

there's a village not very far away. Signs've been more plentiful in the last hour. 'Let's ride up to that ridge before we call it a day."

The two men spurred their horses up the deer track that led to a thickly-wooded ridge ahead of them. They dismounted and made their way cautiously to the top.

Before them stretched a vast valley, broken by small streams and creeks that joined each other to form a tributary of the Coosa River. Ash, oak and birch trees covered the hillsides and spread into the valley on all sides to merge with the willows and rushes that bordered the waterways.

" What's that, Jake?" Davy pointed far to the east where a slight haze showed clearly above the woods.

" Smoke," growled the old hunter. " Several fires by the look of it. Looks like we've found your village after all."

But once again their luck was out. By the time the attacking force reached the village it was deserted. Cooking fires still burned in the clearing and the remains of a meal lay half eaten all around. The Creeks had been warned, and had slipped quietly away into the depths of the forest.

The disgruntled men ransacked the mud huts for food. They found a store of dried beans and stripped the corn cobs from the maize plants. At least they fed well that day, and that was something to ease their disappointment.

They were setting fire to the huts before leaving when George Russell and Luke Peters rode in. They made straight for Davy, and by their expressions he realised they had news.

"You look as perky as a bear with a pot o' honey, young George. What's happened?"

"We've found 'em!"

"Found who?"

"A whole village o' Red Sticks, just sittin' an' waitin' to be taken!"

"An' that ain't all, Davy," broke in Luke. "We know where Tecumseh's main war party is, an' we found out why we couldn't trace him before."

"Now that's really somethin'!" Davy exclaimed. "Don't stand there grinnin' fit to bust. Out with it. Tell me all you know."

George hesitated for a moment to collect his thoughts, and then the words came tumbling out with scarcely a pause.

"It was the Cherokees who put us wise," George began. "Luke an' I slipped back to the village the half-breed took us to on our first trip. The chief told us about this Creek hide-out. It's not more than six miles from here. Then he told us about the White Indian."

"What about him?" Davy asked.

"He fooled us all. His story about Tecumseh crossing at Ten Islands was false. He made it up to scare us away. He sent that messenger to the Cherokee village, an' another to put the major on a false scent. Tecumseh's never been near this territory!"

"Where is he then?"

"Far south, below Ten Islands, sittin' in ambush for the General!"

"Is he, by Heaven!"

"Never did trust that White Indian feller," came the voice of Jake from the far side of the cooking fire where he sat thoughtfully trimming his finger nails with a fearsome hunting knife. " I think you an' me had better pay him a visit, Davy. What d'you say?"

" Later, Jake. We've got enough on our hands for the present. He'll keep. I've got another job for you."

" What's that?" Jake looked up suspiciously.

" Saddle up an' ride like the devil to warn the General. Tell him we're goin' to clean up this party o' Creeks in their village, an' then we'll join him against Tecumseh."

" I might've known it !" snorted the hunter. " Wish I'd kept my big mouth shut." But he got to his feet and made briskly for the horses.

*   *   *

The men were jubilant when they heard the news. The promise of some real action at last buoyed up their flagging spirits. Or perhaps it was the contentment that comes from a full stomach after days of short rations—who knows? The fact remained that the prospect of a further spell of riding, followed by the fury and exertion of an attack, was shrugged off carelessly as though it was of no importance.

" Let's get at 'em, an' the sooner the better," was the general reaction as they prepared for the attack.

Six or seven miles takes little time to travel on a good horse, but it was two hours before they reached their allotted positions, for Davy insisted on a wide sweep round the village. All depended upon surprise, and he was taking no chances of the Red Sticks slipping through the net he proposed to draw around them.

The force split into three soon after leaving the clearing, where the ashes of the Indian huts still smouldered. One party headed east in a wide sweep that would bring them out in a half circle round one side of the village, while another party circled to the west in the same way. Davy and a company of rangers stirred restlessly in their saddles, waiting for the signal that would tell them the two forces had made contact on the far side of the village. When that came, the net would be complete.

" Somethin' must've gone wrong," muttered George Russell after what seemed an age had dragged by without a sound being heard.

" Patience, lad. The longer they take the better. When the time comes stick close by me an' don't take any risks. There's no need for anyone to get hurt if we handle this properly."

Suddenly from the rear of the village came the sound of a single shot, and pandemonium broke loose.

" This is it!" yelled Davy, and the whole company of rangers sprang into action. They rode hard, straight for the slope down to the hollow in which the village lay. They broke through the trees and headed for the largest group of huts.

Scantily clothed red men appeared from all directions, pausing only to grab up bows and arrows, an occasional rifle or a spear. They fired as they ran towards the mounted rangers, the clearing resounding with their war cries. Women and children fled screaming into the huts at the sight of the white men.

The rangers paused as they reached the open. They steadied their mounts while they took aim. Next moment the woods echoed with the roar of a shattering fusillade of shots. The Red Sticks fell like ninepins, but the survivors came on relentlessly.

"Into 'em!" yelled Davy, spurring his horse forward down the slope.

But there was no need for further fighting, for, as the rangers charged, the flanking forces came into sight from the surrounding woods, pouring shot after shot into the village. Caught on all sides the Creeks threw down their arms and begged for mercy.

Out of the corner of his eye Davy saw three fat squaws throw their arms about George Russell's legs as he sat straight and tight-lipped in the saddle, watching the surrendering braves. He saw his young friend try frantically to brush them off, but they clung desperately, pleading for him to take them prisoner.

"This is no time to start courtin', young George," Davy cried, relaxing from the tension of the past few minutes. "Better call Luke to give you a hand. He reckons he's a real lady's man!"

But Davy's amusement came to an abrupt end at George's reply. "Luke'll never give anyone a helpin' hand again, Davy. Take a look up the slope."

Davy turned slowly in his saddle. A crumpled form lay by the side of the track, beneath a riderless horse that nuzzled nervously at its master's face. Four other white men lay close by.

CHAPTER VII

The River Crossing

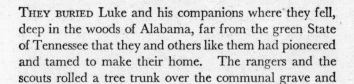

THEY BURIED Luke and his companions where they fell, deep in the woods of Alabama, far from the green State of Tennessee that they and others like them had pioneered and tamed to make their home. The rangers and the scouts rolled a tree trunk over the communal grave and paid their last respects to five brave men before setting out on the long ride to Ten Islands.

"Why did it have to be Luke, of all people?" George Russell protested as he and Davy turned to go. "He wished no harm to anyone."

Davy laid a comforting arm on the young man's shoulders. He sought awkwardly for the right words to express what he felt.

"War's like that, George," he said quietly. "None of us wants it. It's an evil thing. And when it comes it's ordinary decent men like Luke who suffer. Those men gave their lives to stop a crazy madman spreading terror and misery through the land. It's up to us to carry on an' stamp it out for good."

"Perhaps you're right, Davy, but I still can't see why it had to be Luke."

"That's life," said Davy. "None of us knows when our number's goin' to come up. We just have to do what we think right, an' take our chance."

They walked to their horses in silence, then mounted and rode out of the empty village behind their companions and the hundred odd prisoners that they had taken.

Progress was slow, for the mounted men had to check their pace to that of the walking prisoners and the wounded. It was two full days and more before they saw the waters of the Coosa ahead of them. The crossing where the ten small green islands lay in the centre of the wide expanse of water, was out of sight round a bend to the south. Davy led the volunteers to the water's edge and started to head south along the tree-lined river bank when a shout halted him.

"Say! Crockett. Let's cross here. It's easier travelling on the far bank. There ain't so many trees over there."

"Yeah, Davy. Tom's right. The water looks shallow enough here," another voice chimed in, and soon others were agreeing.

Davy paused on the bank and studied the currents and what he could see of the bed of the river.

"Don't like it much," he said at length. "It's shallow enough, but the bottom's rock not gravel, an' there's shoals there I don't like the look of."

"Aw, Crockett, you're too durned particular," came the voice of the first ranger. "I'm goin' in. Don't fancy an extra hour or so in the saddle after all the travellin' we've done in the last few days."

The man rode to the bank, driving his horse forward with a smart slap to its flank. Others moved to follow.

" Watch it, man !" Davy shouted as the horse stepped into the water up to its chest. " Take it slowly or you may be in trouble."

" Aw stop fussin', Crockett. I know what I'm doin'."

" I hope you do, Mr. Know-all," George Russell heard Davy mutter under his breath.

The horse made easy progress through the water until it came to the rough bottom where the shoals began. Here it stumbled, regained its foothold and stepped forward cautiously. The impatient rider gave it another vicious slap to urge it forward. The horse was seen to lurch suddenly sideways, check and then stop. Again the rider slapped it. This time the horse did not respond. It struggled and kicked, lashing the water into an angry foam. A frightened neigh broke from its throat, high-pitched and terrifying.

Davy didn't hesitate. He wheeled his mount and forced his way through the waiting horsemen.

" Get back !" he ordered. " That durned hot-head's got his horse trapped."

Slowly, cautiously, Davy guided his big seventeen-hand gelding forward, allowing it to test each foothold before it transferred its weight from rear hoof to forefoot. As they approached the struggling horse his mount began to shiver with fright. Davy leant forward and spoke soothingly in its ear, coaxing it, lulling its fears. Step by step it pressed ahead until barely six feet separated the two horses.

" Slip out o' the saddle an' swim round to me," Davy ordered quietly. " Leave your reins trailin' on this side. I may need them."

Obediently the now thoroughly frightened man swung his leg over the saddle and slipped into the water while

Davy calmed his horse and held it motionless. He freed his right hand stirrup and bent to grasp the ranger's hand as he swam alongside. A heave and the man was sprawled across the horse's back, his floundering foot searching for the stirrup iron.

"Now ease into my saddle," said Davy as the man clung to his broad shoulders. "I'm goin' in."

"You're crazy, Crockett! You'll be kicked to ribbons. Put a bullet through its head an' let's get back to dry land."

But Davy was already half out of the saddle. "You talk too much," he said bitingly. And in a second he was in the water, striking out to grasp the reins of the trapped horse where they floated on the surface. He seized them and held on while he forced his legs against the swift flowing current until he touched the uneven river bed.

Once he had found a foothold he stood upright and worked his way closer to the struggling horse, keeping a careful eye on the kicking hind-legs. Presently he found himself standing within touch of the trapped foreleg. He spoke softly to the horse all the time; gentle, cooing noises issued from his lips in a steady monotonous stream—and gradually the straining animal calmed and began to nicker and whinny pleadingly.

He reached out and touched the horse, still keeping a firm grip on the rein with his other hand to balance himself against the current. He fondled the trembling animal, still talking and making his gentle noises. He stood there patiently until he felt the soft muzzle brush against the shoulder of his hunting jacket.

A wave of relief passed over him. He had won the

horse's confidence—that was half the battle. Now to free the trapped hoof.

He groped with his moccasined feet until he found the crevice in the rock. He traced its outline until he could picture exactly how it lay. He grasped the foreleg, took a deep breath and slid softly down below the water.

It took five attempts to free the horse. The rock refused to yield to Davy's hunting knife at first, but after the third attempt he struck a small crack or fissure. He prised the blade into the rock, forcing the crack to widen. The cutting edge of the knife chipped and broke, but the main body of the tempered steel remained intact and gradually the rock relaxed its pressure on the hoof.

The horse sprang back, turned abruptly, rearing high above him, and for one horrible moment he thought the flaying forelegs were about to pound him to a pulp. But all was well. The horse continued turning on its hind-legs and came down on all four hooves and hobbled painfully for the bank.

But Davy was not out of trouble. No sooner had he lost the support of the horse's leg than the water surged against his body, beating him back off balance. He felt himself bending at the knees. He overbalanced and struck out strongly for his own horse. He failed to reach it, and the current, surging relentlessly down-stream, carried him with it.

CHAPTER VIII

Tecumseh takes a Beating

———— ⬥⬥⬥ ————

JAKE MARSHALL looked guiltily over his shoulder; saw no one was watching him and stepped into the woods. He made his way quickly to a hickory thicket by the river bank and disappeared from sight.

He chuckled as he settled himself comfortably and prepared for a nice long sleep in the warm midday sun. He felt like a boy playing hookey from school.

Everyone seemed to have forgotten about Jake since he brought news of the impending attack on the Creek village, and the whereabouts of Tecumseh and his war party. General Jackson and his officers were far too busy working out plans and waiting impatiently for reports from scouts to worry about one lone volunteer. Without the rest of Davy's force of mounted scouts Jake was odd man out in the camp at Ten Islands—and it suited him perfectly!

"This is the way to play at soldiers," the old hunter muttered drowsily to no one in particular. "Let them pesky fancy pants o' regulars get on with it." Presently resounding snores began to shake the thicket. Jake dreamt happily of pleasant hours in the tavern at Winchester settlement, yarning with fellow hunters and neighbours.

But his spell of bliss was short-lived. A cry from the river woke him with a start. He sprang to his feet, thinking one of the officers had found him shirking his duties. There was nobody in sight. Puzzled, Jake looked about him, and then his eyes caught a movement upstream. A log floated towards him. It swung close in to the bank as the eddies pushed round the bend in the Coosa. He saw a man's head and a waving arm raised to grasp a protruding branch.

Jake was used to instant decisions. He whipped his heavy hunting knife from its sheath and slashed at the base of the nearest sapling. The green wood tore apart as he put pressure on the trunk. Another slash and it was free.

He was just in time. He thrust the head of the tree out into the water as the log and its human cargo drew level with him.

" Grab hold, feller! " he yelled.

The man seized the leafy branches, kicked the log away from him and pulled himself hand over hand to the shallow water by the bank.

Jake stared in amazement as his bedraggled friend waded ashore. " Well! Burn my britches! If it ain't Davy Crockett! If I'd known it was you I would've let you swim," he exclaimed, but he grasped the chief scout's hand to help him up the bank.

" Thanks Jake. Didn't fancy endin' up down river among Tecumseh and his boys," Davy gasped, sinking to the ground to regain his breath.

" Don't know what you'd do without me," grunted Jake. " This'll teach you to go off after Red Sticks while

I do your dirty work for you. How did the attack go?"

"Cleaned up two hundred o' the critturs," Davy answered, starting to strip his sodden clothes and hang them near the fire that Jake was busy building. "Then some fool got his horse trapped trying to cross the river higher up. That's how I got a wet shirt. The others'll be along shortly."

Jake didn't waste time asking for details—he'd hear them soon enough when the attacking force returned. "The General will be glad to see you," he remarked. "He's been hoppin' about like a flea in a bottle waitin' for news. Can't hardly contain himself, he's that keen to get a crack at Tecumseh."

"He won't have to wait long now," said Davy. "See if you can rustle up some dry clothes for me, Jake, an' I'll put him out of his misery."

*   *   *

General Jackson's lined face broke into a rare smile when he heard Davy's news. "Nice work, Crockett," he said. "That'll give the heathens something to think about. How soon will your boys be rested enough for action again?"

"A good night's sleep'll be enough for them."

"Right. I want them to initiate the attack, while my foot soldiers follow your plan of encirclement. I've had Cherokee scouts out since your message arrived, and we've located Tecumseh. His braves are lying in wait just beyond Fort Taladega."

The plan worked perfectly.

It was late morning when Tecumseh's braves brought

news that the white men were approaching fast, in force. They massed thickly in a sunken gully close to the trail, gleefully preparing for the ambush. A thick belt of sycamores and cottonwoods cast dense shade over their heads as they crouched behind clumps of bracken and the tall grasses of midsummer, waiting with the stolid patience of their race for the signal from their chief.

Presently the sound of marching feet drifted towards them on the still air, and with it came the hoof beats of six hundred horses, the jingle of spurs and the slap of sword and rifle scabbards against saddle-cloths and blankets. Tecumseh's eyes gleamed greedily as he pictured the fine mounts his horseless warriors would own before the day was through.

The column swung into sight down the trail, with Jackson and his senior officers at the head. Close behind rode Davy and his scouts, rifles cradled in their arms, eyes alert but bodies relaxed and swaying to the rhythm of their horses.

Behind them followed the company of mounted rangers, and at their rear the foot soldiers and volunteers filled the trail, packed eight deep in row upon row.

Tecumseh ran his tongue over thin lips. There must be fifteen hundred white men there, he thought, all fully armed and equipped—and hurrying to their death, totally unaware of the eleven hundred warriors who lay in wait for them.

But Tecumseh was wrong.

The General knew exactly where the Red Sticks lay. His Cherokees had drawn a map in the dust of the trail before he left Ten Islands, marking the very spot Tecumseh had chosen, and the number of his braves. Jackson laughed silently to himself as he thought of the surprise in store for the Creeks.

The plan had been rehearsed until every man in the force knew what he had to do. There was no need for a single command or signal. At a prearranged spot where the trail narrowed and the trees were thickest, the column of foot soldiers split into two, branching left and right into the woods. The horses of the rangers in front of them shielded their movements completely. Once in the woods, they took to their heels and ran to outflank the unsuspecting Red Sticks, while the mounted men rode on towards the gully.

"This is the spot," whispered Jackson to the Colonel who rode beside him. They swung their horses suddenly off the trail, and Davy and his scouts went into action.

Letting loose a battle cry of his own, he urged his horse into a gallop, straight for the gully. The horsemen spread out around him. Steel-shod hooves bit into the packed earth of the trail. A cloud of dust billowed skywards as they streamed to the attack.

Tecumseh lost his head. He sprang into sight, his brilliant head-dress flashing in the bright sunlight, and from the gully poured his screaming warriors.

Davy smiled grimly. The plan was working like a charm. He held his horse at the gallop until the bulk of Tecumseh's warriors were in the open, then he thrust his rifle high above his head in signal.

The charging scouts reined to a rearing halt behind him, flung themselves from the saddle and dived for cover among the trees. As the riderless horses whirled and ran back up the trail, rifle after rifle blasted out its song of death, the bullets scything through the leading red men.

They paused among their dead, then raced forward again, straight for the hated white men, letting loose a cloud of arrows as they ran.

A second volley tore into them, and they broke. They sprang for the cover of the woods, only to be met by a blistering fusillade from the foot volunteers who waited for them. They panicked, running back and forth across the trail, bewildered, not knowing in which direction safety lay, and all the time the leaden bullets rained into them from all sides.

Fear-crazed, the Red Sticks tore back down the gully, only to find they had been encircled. Again a volley of shots blazed at them from the trees, but in desperation the survivors pressed on until they came to grips with the soldiers. They fought hand to hand, their rifles and bows cast aside. They fought like wild beasts, with only one thought in their heads—to get out of this death trap and into the security of the woods. By sheer force of numbers they broke the line of riflemen and ran howling to safety, leaving five hundred of their fellows lying motionless beneath the blue haze of gun-smoke.

Tecumseh's dreams were shattered. The settlers of Fort Mimms had been avenged.

CHAPTER IX

The General and the Scout

THE VICTORY at Fort Taladega was the beginning of the end for Tecumseh. His warriors never forgot the beating they had received from Jackson's army, and although the war continued for many months the Red Sticks confined their activities to minor skirmishes and night attacks. They struck suddenly from dense cover, and then retreated, never giving the horsemen time to engage them nor a chance to outmanœuvre them. Tecumseh had learnt his lesson.

But victory over one enemy brought with it the realisation that yet another enemy had to be defeated. An army and its prisoners have to eat, and Jackson's men found their rations dwindling day by day. They watched the river anxiously for signs of the supply boats that were long overdue. They found their corn stocks exhausted and beans non-existent.

Fights broke out among the soldiers and the volunteers —senseless fights over the size of a portion of meat or a hoarded coffee ration. They scoured the country round Ten Islands for food, and many men fell victims to scalping parties that caught them as they hunted too far from camp.

Jake Marshall had real cause for grumbling now, and he made the most of it.

"Sufferin' bob-cats!" he snarled, looking at the meagre ration of food that lay unappetisingly on his wooden platter. "There ain't enough here to feed a black beetle! An' what is it? Can you answer me that, fellers?" He prodded the mess suspiciously with his knife.

"Looks like rattlesnake stew to me," suggested George Russell. "That cook was mighty careful no one watched him when he made it."

"No use grumblin'," said Davy, swallowing his ration in one mouthful and trying hard to suppress a grimace of distaste. "We'll have to work out some way o' feedin' ourselves. We shan't be fit to fight if this goes on much longer."

"Well, think up some way quick," Jake grunted, "or my backbone'll soon be showin' through my belly."

"When I think of those corn patches we burnt at the Creek villages, I could kick myself," muttered George, half to himself. "We took what was ready, but the rest o' the crop would've been ripe by now."

"Jumpin' cats!" burst out Davy suddenly. "Why on earth didn't I think o' that before?"

"What?"

"The White Indian!"

"What in blazes has the White Indian got to do with my empty belly?" asked Jake scornfully. "You ain't been out in the sun without a hat, have you, Davy?"

"But don't you remember? That barn alongside his

cabin was stacked full o' beans an' he had a mighty fine crop o' corn growin' in the clearing!"

"Well, I'll go to sea!" exclaimed Jake. "O' course! An' besides, we owe that crittur one for spinning lyin' yarns."

The three men were on their feet now, so great was their excitement. They all started talking at once.

"We'll need several pack horses," said George.

"An' plenty o' deerskin pouches," said Jake.

"And permission from the General," said Davy soberly.

"That'll be all right. You go see him while we get the kit sorted out, an' commandeer the horses. He'll listen to you."

Jake was right. General Jackson welcomed the idea. He was at his wits' end to find some way of feeding the men in his command. "Go as soon as you like, Crockett," he said. "Take what horses and men you need, but be careful. You and your men are the eyes and ears of my army. I can't afford to lose any of you."

They set out within the hour, riding north to Ditto's Crossing. There they made camp for the night and were in the saddle long before dawn, following the track they had taken on their first excursion into Indian Territory. They travelled fast, stopping for nothing, and by late afternoon they caught sight of the little homestead ahead of them.

"Watch the horses, George, while Jake an' I have a sniff around," ordered Davy, throwing the reins to his young friend.

The two men crept forward carefully, slipping from

cover to cover, their eyes fixed on the cabin. There was no sign of life.

"No horses in the pasture," Davy muttered.

"No smoke, neither," growled Jake. "Let's take a chance, anyway."

They broke cover and, rifles at the ready, approached the cabin. They eased through the rails of the pasture fence, skirted the barn and within minutes were peering in at the windows of the deserted cabin.

All was quiet, and from what they saw when they stepped through the doorway the White Indian had been gone for some days. They made their way to the barn. That too was empty.

"Looks like we've come on a fool's errand," said Jake despondently.

"But what's happened to that food?" asked Davy. "They can't have taken it all away. Besides it looks as though they left in a hurry. There's the remains of a meal on the table in the cabin. I reckon it's been cached away close and handy."

They called George Russell up, and together the three men began a search of the surrounding woods. They soon came upon a well-worn path through the trees which led them to the base of a rock outcrop. There they found a natural cave, stacked high with food of every kind. Corn, beans, maize, potatoes and even dried haunches of meat filled the cool recesses of the cave. It made a perfect storehouse.

Jake's eyes lit up in wonder. He licked his lips hungrily. "Me for a meal before we do any work!" he exclaimed.

"You're durned right," agreed both George and Davy, grinning with delight at their find. They took enough for a full scale banquet and returned gleefully to the cabin to cook it. It took little time for the hungry men to light a fire, and soon the tantalizing smell of a wholesome stew rose up from the hearth.

They were wolfing the food noisily when the sound of horses' hooves disturbed them. They ducked out of sight, reaching for their rifles, thanking their stars that they had taken the horses into the shade out of sight from the trail.

" It's the White Indian's sons," Davy whispered, peering round the open door. " Let 'em get into range, then I'll give 'em a warnin' shot."

" Tell me when you're ready, Davy," chuckled Jake, reaching up to the table above him to grab a handful of food. " No pesky half-breed's goin' to stop me finishing this meal." He stuffed the food into his mouth and chewed away happily, regardless of the gravy that trickled greasily down his unshaven chin.

Davy's shot stopped the two horsemen in their tracks. They held their hands high as the scouts stepped through the doorway, rifles levelled.

" Get off those horses an' drop your knives on the ground," Davy ordered.

The half-breeds sullenly obeyed.

" What do you want with us?" the taller of the two asked. " We are your friends. You have no right to enter our home."

" Friends, he says!" snorted Jake at Davy's elbow. " You ain't no friend o' mine, you twistin' rattler."

Davy pointed up the track to the cave. " Get on up that path, an' look lively. We've got work for you."

" What are you goin' to make them do, Davy?" asked George Russell.

"You'll see, son. Come and watch the fun."

The three scouts followed their prisoners to the cave, and there George found the answer to his question. Davy indicated the pack horses tethered close by. "I want those packs filled and loaded, within the hour," he said briefly. The half-breeds protested violently but in vain. They saw the chief scout's rifle rising up to bear directly at them, and they turned resignedly and went to work.

The three scouts settled themselves comfortably on a bed of moss that carpeted the rocks, watching idly as the store was stripped of every ounce of food it contained.

Jake Marshall spluttered with laughter as he lolled happily against a tree, his fur hat tilted forward to shade his eyes from the sun. He squinted at George and winked solemnly. "Ain't felt so contented in years," he chuckled.

Davy smiled slowly. "There's more to come, Jake," he drawled.

"What d'you mean, Davy?" the old hunter looked suspiciously at his friend. "What have you got up your sleeve?"

"Nothin' much. I only thought the General would appreciate it if we brought him back two more volunteers than we left camp with."

Jake slapped his thigh, and roared with laughter. "If that don't beat all!" he gurgled. "*Volunteers* you say! Can't wait to see their faces when you tell 'em they've volunteered themselves into the Army without knowin' it!"

*   *   *

Davy and his private supply column rode into camp to

be met with a reception fit for royalty. The hungry men clustered round them vying with each other for the job of unloading the bulging packs. As the last of the food was being lifted down, one of the soldiers sidled up to Davy. "I'll give you ten dollars for a haunch o' that meat," he whispered slyly.

The hunter looked the man up and down with contempt. He reached out, took him by the ear and marched him off to the cooks, who were already hard at work over their fires. "Take a good look at this skunk," he snapped. "See that he gets served last of all. If he or any other varmint tries to bribe you for more than his share, let me know an' I'll deal with him."

That night, around the camp-fires the volunteers grouped themselves happily, singing songs from their native lands, exchanging tall stories of previous Indian fighting, or highly exaggerated hunting tales. And as the conversation flowed, the name of Davy Crockett kept recurring.

"That Crockett's a real straight feller," came a voice from one group. "Did you hear what he told the cooks this afternoon?"

"Yeah," answered another voice. "But what about the way he saved that horse at the ford the other day? He doesn't give a tinker's cuss for anyone or anything once he's made up his mind what's right."

"Zeb Harriss was tellin' me Davy gave him his own ration the other day when he was sick," a third man broke in. "An' when we were out in the woods last week he told us yarns that made us crack our sides with laughin'. He's one o' the best an' no mistake."

But Davy himself was strangely quiet. He sat apart

from his companions, staring into the fire as though lost in a dream. He looked up and smiled as George Russell strolled towards him.

"What's on your mind, Davy?" the young man asked quietly.

"Oh, just thinkin', son."

"What about, if it ain't personal?"

Davy looked at his young friend affectionately. "It is kinda personal, George," he said. "But there ain't no cause for secrets among friends. I was thinkin' about Polly an' my boys. We told 'em we'd only be gone a week or two, an' now the weeks have grown into months, an' there don't seem any end to it."

George nodded. "I've been thinkin' the same, Davy. I'm feelin' homesick too, an' there's plenty o' the boys feel the same way."

Jake appeared from one of the groups of men as they talked. He caught sight of them and ambled over to sit with them.

"Hear there's a new bunch o' volunteers on its way from Tennessee, Davy," he grunted, "'bout the same number as we muster."

Davy brightened up. "Is that definite?" he asked eagerly.

"Sure as I'm sittin' here."

"In that case my mind's made up," Davy said emphatically.

"How do you mean?"

"I'm goin' back home straight away," said Davy.

*　　　*　　　*

General Jackson was furious.

"You men can't go back until I say so!" he thundered. "You're under Army discipline, and Army orders. I need you here and I'll see you don't leave."

Davy flushed, and George and Jake, who stood among the spokesmen for the volunteers, knew that his dander was up.

"This is where friend Hickory Face gets told off good and proper," whispered Jake.

"Now see here General Jackson. We ain't soldiers. We're volunteers. We've got wives an' families to look after, our business to see to, an' farms to run. We dropped everything to slam Tecumseh, an' now that's done we're goin' home. We signed on for a sixty-day hitch, an' now three months have gone. Our clothes are worn out, our horses lame, an' the Army can't feed us. We're goin' whether you like it or not."

"If you try and leave this camp against my orders, Crockett, I'll have you shot!"

That did it. Davy's eyes glinted with cold, ruthless anger. He stared the General straight in the eyes for a long time.

"Then you an' I are goin' to fall out, right here an' now, General," he said at length, every word uttered slowly and distinctly so that all the volunteers could hear. "I'm going, an' I'm takin' the boys with me. There are reinforcements due here any time now an' they'll take over from us. We'll sign on for another hitch if you need us—but only when we're good an' ready."

He turned and stalked away from the General's tent, his eyes blazing. "Come on, boys!" he yelled. "Pick up your kit an' saddle up."

Jackson was nearly purple in the face. He swung round to his regular officers. " Muster your men around the camp!" he roared. " Shoot the first man that tries to leave!"

The regulars, trained to obey without question, fell in at the double. They primed their rifles and stood awaiting the next move on the part of the volunteers.

" Get on with it, boys," said Davy calmly, tightening his girth strap. " We're comin' through."

Their reins looped over their arms, the volunteers headed for the line of regulars. They walked slowly forward, and at a word from Davy the click of rifle hammers rattled through their ranks as each man brought his weapon to full cock.

Davy kept his eyes fixed on the face of a burly sergeant who stood rigidly at his post, straight in front of him. To his surprise he saw the man's right eyelid drop in a slow, deliberate wink. As he drew level the sergeant stepped aside.

" Good luck, Davy," he said with a smile. " Shan't forget that meal you gave us in a hurry!"

Right down the line the regulars made way for the volunteers and their horses, while General Jackson stood speechless in the empty camp.

CHAPTER X

Colonel Crockett

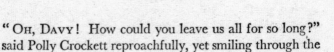

"Oh, Davy! How could you leave us all for so long?" said Polly Crockett reproachfully, yet smiling through the tears of joy at her husband's safe return. Davy kissed her tenderly.

"I had to fight the whole army and a turkey-cock of a General to get back to you, my dear," he said with a twinkle in his eyes. "But it was worth it."

"That old General sounds horrible," said Polly, vehemently.

"He's no worse than most o' the regulars," said Davy. "He's a good soldier. I wonder how he'll treat me when I get back?"

"Get back?" Polly whirled round from the fire where she was busily cooking his favourite meal. "You're not thinking of going back, Davy?"

"'Fraid so, Polly."

"But you can't. I won't let you! You've done your share, and more by all accounts."

"I gave my word, Polly. I don't want to go, but a feller's got to finish a job once he starts it. I shan't rest easy till the Creeks are buttoned up for good."

Despite Polly's arguing and pleading with him, Davy stuck to his decision. Once his mind was made up there was no shifting him. At length Polly grew resigned to his return.

"Well, if you *are* going to join that dreadful Army again, Davy, I'll make certain you go properly clothed for the winter," she said one night, and next morning her needle flew as she stitched at a brand-new hunting jacket and a warm suit of homespun cloth. She fed him up until his cheeks filled out to their normal roundness.

She made him fashion new leggings and spare moccasins out of stout leather. She packed him up a supply of dried meats and biscuits, and when the day of his return came, she saw him off with a brave smile.

To tell the truth, although he hated leaving his family, Davy was looking forward to a further spell of scouting for the Army. There was something about the need for field-craft, and the pitting of his wits against the wily Red Sticks that appealed to him. It was so like bear hunting, he thought to himself as he rode off to meet Jake Marshall, who was to accompany him again.

"Thought you'd had enough o' the Army, Jake?" he chaffed the old hunter as they rode together into Winchester. "I believe you liked it all the time."

"Maybe," admitted Jake grudgingly. "Perhaps I do. To tell the truth, Davy, I get mighty lonesome up in the woods sometimes. There ain't no one to grumble at, an' that don't do at all!"

A strong bond of friendship had developed between the two men in the past campaign, and the months that were to follow drew them closer together than ever. They were inseparable. Jake became known throughout the Army as " Crockett's shadow," and he secretly delighted in the nickname.

Together they joined a special spy company that had been formed in their absence. They found themselves under the command of old Major Russell of Tennessee— a man they both knew and respected. With him they served loyally and happily right through the second hitch of duty.

They played a big part in the desperate battle at the Horse Shoe Bend of the Talapoosa. They fought together in many a skirmish and night attack and when Davy volunteered for further service with the southern forces based on the old site of Fort Mimms, Jake accompanied him.

Davy's reputation grew all the time. Both officers and men relied on him, trusting his judgment while respecting him for his ability, his unfailing good humour and his great good heart. He was welcome in every camp.

At the end of his third tour of duty Davy returned home for good—or so he thought.

" I've had enough o' fightin', Jake," he said to his old friend as they rode slowly homewards through the lands they had fought to free from Tecumseh's rule. " The war will be over in a matter o' months now. We've done our duty, an' no one can say fairer than that."

" What are you thinkin' o' doin' Davy?" asked Jake. " Can't see you settlin' down at Bean Creek. Got any ideas?"

" I'm headin' West again. From what I hear, Obion River territory's the place for me. The land o' the Chick-asaws they call it. Plenty o' game an' the woods swarmin' with bear. What more can a man ask for?"

They parted at Winchester. Jake had business of his own to see to up-country where his relatives had settled, while Davy was impatient to get back to his family and prepare for the move.

But fate had other plans in store for the kindly hunter. His fame had travelled ahead of him, spreading far and wide throughout the State of Tennessee. Men talk when they get together after months in the backwoods, and as the volunteers and militia men drifted back from the wars, the name of Davy Crockett became a household word. Settlers meeting in the taverns or at the frolics at harvest time, heard the story of his stand against General Jackson, and many more tales of his courage and skill.

The stories penetrated to the depths of the Obion River country, where Davy hunted bear, oblivious of the things that were being said about him on every hand. Jake Marshall heard the talk, and added to the legends that were building up around his friend's name. One day he rode up to the Crockett homestead with news.

"Now you've done it, Davy," he growled.

"Done what?"

"Got yourself elected to the Tennessee Legislature!" said Jake with a grin.

"What in blue blazes are you talkin' about, Jake?"

"Just what I say. The settlers want you to represent them, so they put your name forward an' you've been elected. Thought you ought to know!"

"But I don't know anythin' about laws an' suchlike," Davy protested.

"You didn't know anythin' about Indian fightin', but you learnt pretty quick," said Jake, dryly. "First meetin'

falls on the third o' the month. You'd better be there—
the folks are countin' on you."

Davy went to that meeting and suddenly found himself
in a different world. He was fascinated with what he saw
and heard. He brought a fresh eye and a clear brain to
the problems of politics, and before he knew what was
happening had become a figure of importance.

"But I ain't had no schoolin' worth talkin' about!" he
exclaimed to Polly one day when the news came through
that he had been made a magistrate for the district as
well.

"What's the matter?" asked Polly. "You know what's
right and what's wrong. That's all you need to give a
fair verdict. The men and women here have faith in you.
I know you won't let them down."

Davy didn't let them down. He mastered his responsibilities, brushing up his reading and writing sufficiently
to fill up the legal forms and to record his decisions. He
dealt fairly and mercifully with the men who came before
him—and he was happy. He had found a new interest,
and a new outlook on life.

But his proudest moment was when the settlers met to
form a local militia force. Without hesitation the volunteers voted unanimously for Davy Crockett's name to go
forward as their Colonel.

Jake Marshall laughed uproariously when he heard the
news. "Colonel Crockett!" he spluttered. "Now I've
heard everythin'! After what you've said about fool Captains, Majors an' Colonels, friend Davy, I never thought
I'd live to see the day when you became one yourself!"

But Jake, and Davy himself, had more surprises in
store.

Elections were held to choose a representative to go to Washington and take his seat in the House of Congress —the Government of the American people. Davy let his name be entered as a candidate, not dreaming that he stood a chance.

Within days he found himself elected. The hunter from the backwoods had become a national figure.

CHAPTER XI

Congressman Crockett

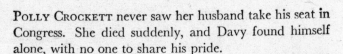

POLLY CROCKETT never saw her husband take his seat in Congress. She died suddenly, and Davy found himself alone, with no one to share his pride.

Blinded by grief, he buried himself in work for the settlers he represented. He fought tooth and nail against the unfair land laws that threatened to drive the homesteaders from their properties. He ranted and raved at the politicians who proposed to break the treaties that had ended the Creek war. No cause was too small, nor the outcome too uncertain. If he felt sure that he was right, no man could sway him.

His drawling, unpolished speech came to be feared by his opponents, for his tongue lashed them unmercifully. He had no time for pomposity and fine-sounding phrases. His words were short, his manner direct and forceful. He spoke for the ordinary people of an undeveloped State— and he defended their rights with all the strength at his command.

His political rivals laughed at him behind his back, sneering at his rough manners, and uncouth speech. They called him the " Coonskin Congressman," and made fun of his humble origin. But there were many more who admired and respected the tall hunter from the backwoods.

Restless as always, Davy toured the whole of the eastern States, meeting the people, studying their customs and wondering at the undreamed-of sights. He rode on a train for the first time, as excited as a schoolboy at the new experience. He stared in awe at the great cities of the coast with their tall, stone buildings. He watched the great ships sail into the ports, laden with merchandise from countries he hardly knew existed.

Everywhere he went he found himself welcome. When he reached Philadelphia a banquet was given in his honour, and the mayor presented him with a specially made rifle.

"Now that's what I call a rifle!" Davy exclaimed when he saw it. "Ain't never handled a better."

"I don't expect you have, Colonel Crockett," beamed the mayor. "We had it made to your measurements by the finest craftsman in America."

"This is more than a rifle, Mr. Mayor," said Davy, testing the faultless balance, while his eyes admired the beautiful workmanship that had gone to the fashioning of the long barrel, and the engraved walnut of the stock. "This will be a friend as well as a weapon."

"A good friend needs a good name," smiled the mayor, jokingly.

"You're durned right! I'll call her 'Long Betsy,' an' every time I fire her I'll think o' the good people o' Philadelphia."

*　　　*　　　*

"The frontier's on the move, Jake," Davy said to his friend on one of his rare visits to Winchester and the surrounding country. "They tell me the West is opening up with a rush. They're settlin' all along the far bank o' the Mississippi now. Some o' the richest land in America by all accounts."

"Grow anythin' you like, as easy as fallin' off a log," Jake agreed. "Cotton, corn, wheat, barley, tobacco— every mortal thing. But where's this Texas place the Government keeps talkin' about. What sort o' territory is that, an' what's the trouble all about?"

Davy paused. He had been hoping Jake would ask him those very questions. He had heard a lot more than most about this new land, far to the south-west. Strange tales had filtered through to Washington—tales of a land of milk and honey, of the finest grazing pastures that man had ever set eyes on. Great herds of strange animals the settlers called buffalo were said to roam at will in their thousands. Wild horses filled the prairies and wild-eyed, longhorn cattle fattened on the rich grasses. There was talk of mineral wealth, rich deposits of silver, lead and iron—even the magic name "gold" had been mentioned. Something of this he told Jake in answer to his questions.

"Seems this country o' Texas is so rich that everyone wants to own it," Davy went on. "The settlers have been building up their herds an' raising such fine crops that the Mexicans are tryin' to grab hold o' their land for themselves. There's goin' to be trouble down in Texas before we're much older."

Jake sat quietly for several minutes, turning over in his mind what Davy had told him. "Sounds quite a place," he said at length. "When are you aimin' to start?"

Davy looked up in surprise. "Start? What d'you mean, Jake? I ain't said anythin' about goin' down to Texas."

Jake smiled. "You ain't *said* as much. But I know as well as you do that's what you've got at the back o' your mind."

"But I can't, Jake. I've been put up for election to Congress again. If they vote me in for another spell, there's no hope o' gettin' away."

"*If* they vote you in," said Jake.

"Well, it's more than likely," Davy said, modestly.

"Don't you be too sure, friend. General Jackson's President o' the United States now. He ain't never forgotten the way you stood up to him. You mark my words, Davy. You've got a fight on your hands, an' the cards are stacked against you. If Jackson can work it so you don't get elected, he'll die happy."

"We'll see, Jake. But if I don't get in this time, we'll both head for Texas an' find out what this trouble's all about."

"Suits me," said Jake. "I shall be prayin' for you to lose!"

CHAPTER XII

The Call of Texas

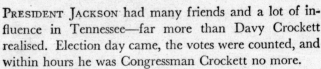

PRESIDENT JACKSON had many friends and a lot of influence in Tennessee—far more than Davy Crockett realised. Election day came, the votes were counted, and within hours he was Congressman Crockett no more.

Davy tried hard to hide his disappointment, he felt the defeat bitterly. It was as though the men and women for whom he had worked so hard had lost their faith in him and cast him aside like a worn-out glove.

"You got your wish, Jake," he said ruefully when the result was announced. "Looks like we're headed for Texas after all."

"Best thing that ever happened," replied Jake gruffly. "Never could get used to havin' a Congressman for a friend. It'll do you the world o' good to get right away from these parts an' strike out fresh for yourself. You're too honest for politics anyway."

Davy shrugged his shoulders. He glanced at the old hunter and smiled. The answering smile came so readily and with such warmth that suddenly he lost his bitterness. He felt the worries and responsibilities of the past years fall from him like a discarded coat. At long last he was free to do what he liked, go where he chose and say and think just what he wanted. His children were grown up now—his affairs were all in order. He was foot-loose and fancy-free!

He looked down at his tailored city clothes and then at Jake's battered old hunting garb.

"The first thing I'm goin' to do is get into some *man's* clothes for a change!" he exclaimed: "Never did feel right in this get-up."

"Now you're talkin'!" said Jake enthusiastically. "A good day's huntin' is what you need. Then off we go to take a squint at these Lexincan critturs you were tellin' me about."

"Mexicans, Jake. Not Lexincans!"

"Lot o' rogues, whatever you call 'em," said Jake.

*   *   *

It was early November when they set out on their long journey. It was a bleak, cold day, the keen wind whip-ping the waters of the Obion into angry foam. Heavy rain-charged clouds lay blackly over the treetops—omin-ous and threatening. But their spirits were high. They felt a thrill of adventure stirring their blood. They were off to see new lands, to make new friends. They had no idea what lay before them and even if they had, it is more than likely that they would have gone just the same.

"D'you mean to say I've got to trust myself to one o' them contraptions?" asked Jake suspiciously when he first set eyes on the flat-bottomed river-boat that was to take them on the first stage of their journey.

"Safe as houses," Davy assured him, adding with a sly

grin, " that is if the current don't run us on to the rocks, or the water don't come aboard, or we don't lose the steering oar."

" You're mighty free with your ' don'ts,' " said Jake, stepping gingerly into the ungainly craft as nervously as though he was swinging into the saddle of an unbroken stallion. " Rather take a ride on a grizzly than float down river in one o' these."

But all went well. The keel-less boat was pushed off and they were away from the bank into the racing waters. Heavily laden with settlers and their livestock it rode the current smoothly, responding sluggishly to the stout beechwood steering oar that jutted out from the square stern. When they came to a bend in the river all hands ran to help the helmsman, straining at the oar to keep the boat from slewing into the river bank.

Down the flooding Obion they sped to the rowdy songs of the boatmen. They passed little settlements and lonely homesteads, tucked away among the trees that lined the river. They shouted cheerfully to families who waved back as they passed, and they jeered derisively at the crews of slower boats as they caught up with them. Davy and Jake began to enjoy themselves. They felt like school-boys who had been let out of school unexpectedly.

Dressed in new suits of fringed buckskin, hats made of whole coonskins, and supple, beaded moccasins they re-clined on the flat roof of the cabin and studied the country through which they passed.

Almost before they realised it they had reached their destination, a small landing stage from which they could cut through the wood to Mill's Point on the Mississippi where the great tall-funnelled paddle-steamers called to drop cargo and pick up passengers. Shouldering their light-weight packs, the two men picked up their rifles and stepped ashore.

They set out at a steady pace, taking the winding trail through the trees. The farther up the trail they went, the richer grew the country. Leafless oaks and sycamores spread their branches wide above them, jostling the inter-lacing boughs of ash and beech for pride of place. Below, shiny-leaved evergreen shrubs grew profusely in the shade, while dense thickets of hickory and nut were everywhere.

There was sign of game wherever Davy cast his eyes. As they progressed towards the high ground he became as restless as a chipmunk. They were passing a cane-brake when Davy suddenly leapt to the side of the trail and bent to examine some tracks in the mud.

" Bear !" he shouted.

" Davy Crockett ! Just you get back on that trail. This is no time to go traipsing off after bears." Jake's voice rang out with dreadful clarity in the still air.

Davy looked up at him sheepishly. " Sorry, Jake," he grinned. " It's been so long since I went huntin' that I just can't resist tearin' off after Brother Bear every time I spot his tracks."

" Well, you tear off up that trail for a change," grunted Jake, glancing apprehensively at the rain-clouds low above them. " We're goin' to get wet shirts if we don't put a jerk into it."

The storm broke as they arrived at the jetty. They ran up the gang-plank on to the wide, holystoned deck of the steamer, and darted into the cover of the ornate saloon. Jake cast his eyes around in open-mouthed wonder. He had never seen such luxuriant furniture or fittings.

Thick pile carpets covered the floor of the room. Polished brass hand-rails gleamed brightly in the light of the many oil lamps that cast shadows over the red plush cushions of the seats that lined the walls. Uniformed negro stewards threaded their way through the crowded passengers with trays of drinks and refreshments.

" It's like a palace! " he muttered to Davy.

" You want to see the White House at Washington," said his friend. " It makes this room look shabby. But I must say I feel a little out o' place standin' around with a rifle in my hand."

" Me too," agreed Jake, stepping gently towards a shadowed corner, as though fearful of spoiling the carpet.

They leaned against the wall and watched the people who were to be their fellow passengers on the long trip to the mouth of the Arkansas. Wealthy planters from the southern states sat talking to elegant, expensively-dressed ladies. Eastern business men doffed their top hats courteously to acquaintances, or huddled close together over business deals. Southern dandies gazed admiringly at their reflections in the huge, gilt-framed mirrors. They cast haughty glances at the buckskin-clad hunters who had joined them, then turned away, ignoring their presence.

Davy felt his colour mounting. He had grown used to public acclaim and respect in the past few years, and he felt the insulting stares bitterly. He turned to Jake and whispered in his ear. Jake listened carefully and a smile spread slowly over his face, until he was grinning from ear to ear.

" I'll do it! " he chuckled. " Just for the fun of it."

He ambled over to a table in the centre of the room, at which sat a fat, prosperous-looking man of aristocratic

bearing who had deliberately turned his back on the frontiersmen while making loud-voiced remarks about
" having to mix with riff-raff on the river-boats these
days."

Jake reached the table and tapped the man on the
shoulder.

" My friend would like you to take refreshment with
him," he stated loudly.

" Then you can tell your friend to go to blazes!" the
man roared. " I'll thank him to keep himself to himself."

" Davy!" Jake called across the room. " This here
feller don't think you're good enough to drink with."

" Is that so?" drawled Davy, stepping into the light.
" Then perhaps I'd better make him change his mind."

In three long paces he crossed the room to the table.
He placed one moccasined foot on an empty chair and
looked earnestly into the startled man's face, Long Betsy
pointed at his heart.

" So you refuse to drink with Colonel Crockett, do
you?" he asked quietly.

" Colonel Crockett!" the man spluttered. " Why, I
had no idea you were the famous Colonel. My apologies,
sir. I had no intention. . . ."

" You had no intention o' mixin' with ' riff-raff,' "
Davy broke in. " Is that what you were goin' to say?"

The man turned two shades paler. A crowd had collected round the table, Davy's name passing from mouth
to mouth.

" It's Colonel Crockett!"

" That must be the famous Long Betsy."

" He's the Coonskin Congressman."

"That's Davy Crockett. Shouldn't like to be in the fat feller's shoes!"

Davy waited for the buzz of conversation to die down. He still kept his rifle pointing at the man, the barrel held unwaveringly in his big hands.

"I think perhaps you're right after all," he drawled at length. "I don't think I *want* you to drink with me. We'll all drink with *you* instead. Steward! Serve refreshments for everyone at this kind gentleman's expense!"

A roar of laughter greeted his words, and Davy soon found himself the centre of an admiring throng who pressed forward to speak to him and shake his hand.

"Is it true you killed a hundred and three bears in eight months, Colonel Crockett?" asked a pretty young girl.

"Hundred an' five," Davy corrected her.

"My! What did you do with them all?"

"Never could figure what to do with them, ma'am," he answered with a sly grin. "We stacked 'em up behind the cabin, painted 'em blue an' now they call that pile o' bears the Blue Ridge o' Tennessee!"

"Is it a hard life in the backwoods, Colonel?" asked a studious-looking man as the laughter died down.

Davy pretended to think the question over carefully for a full minute. "Depends how you look at it, son," he said at last. "You've got to be able to run like an Indian, swim like an alligator, fight like a bob-cat an' wrestle like a bear."

"You're forgettin' somethin'," broke in Jake's voice from the back of the crowd.

"What's that, Jake?"

"You've got to boast like a hunter," said the old man.

Davy laughed. "Trouble with me is I'm talkin' too much, an' not lookin' after my thirst," he said, pushing his way to the bar that stretched across one end of the room. He picked up a tankard of ale and raised it high above his head.

"A toast, ladies and gentlemen!" he called. "To the Wild Frontier."

"The Wild Frontier!" cried the passengers, draining their glasses with a flourish.

CHAPTER XIII

The Gambler

———————⟨≈⟩———————

A NEGRO STEWARD stepped down the companionway from the deck and hurried towards them.

"Colonel Crockett, sah?" he asked respectfully.

"The same," Davy acknowledged.

"The Captain's compliments, Colonel. Will you honour him with your company on the bridge?"

"My thanks to the Captain. My friend an' I will be delighted to join him," Davy replied.

They finished their drinks and made their way to the deck, and from there up the steep steps that led to the bridge. The captain of the river-boat greeted them with great courtesy, taking Davy's hand in a firm grip, and shaking it warmly.

"This is indeed a pleasure, Colonel!" he cried. "I have admired your courage from afar, but I never thought I should have the honour of meeting you in person."

"You're too kind," Davy murmured formally and then introduced Jake.

"Fine ship you've got here," Jake growled. "But it looks as though your chimneys could do with a good sweepin'." He pointed to the twin funnels that towered above them, sending great plumes of black smoke skywards as the stokers piled wood on the fires in preparation for departure.

The captain laughed. "Those are the funnels, Mr. Marshall," he explained.

"Call 'em what you like. A chimney's a chimney the whole world over. I'd sack my cook if he wasted firin' like that!"

It took the captain and Davy the best part of ten minutes to try and explain that the funnels were the smoke stacks of the boiler furnaces, and that the ship was in fact driven by steam.

"Don't believe you," Jake said flatly. "You're pullin' my leg. We'd all be blown sky high if anyone was fool enough to play about with steam boilers in a boat."

"Have it your own way, Jake," said Davy at last. "Come an' have a look at the river. You sure can get a good view of it from here."

The storm had blown itself out, and now the sun shone through the clouds, forming a gigantic rainbow arch over their heads. The mighty Mississippi stretched almost as far as they could see. The water was thick and yellow with the particles of soil and silt it carried from the States through which it passed on its journey south from the source many hundreds of miles away, close to the Canadian border. It flowed sedately by, untroubled and serene.

"That's a powerful lot o' water," said Jake in wonder. "More like an ocean than a river."

"That's what we river-men call it sometimes," agreed the captain. "The inland ocean. If you get caught in a storm when you're out in mid-stream it's for all the world as though you were in the middle of the Atlantic, thousands of miles from land."

"What's that feller doin' down there?" asked Davy, pointing to the bow of the boat. The captain followed the direction of his arm and smiled.

"He's one of the river-boat gamblers," he answered. "We get a few each trip. Some swindle with cards, some with dice, and others, like our friend there, play 'Rig and Thimble' for money."

"Seems to have a pretty flourishin' business," muttered Davy, watching the men who clustered round the gambler to try their luck. "I think I'll go an' join them, if you'll excuse me leavin' you, Captain."

"By all means, Colonel. But he won't let you win more than once."

Davy made his way across the deck to where the gambler sat astride a packing case. He was a well-built man of around Davy's age, sharp-featured, bright-eyed, and debonair. His light grey frock-coat, tight-fitting trousers, and embroidered waistcoat were all of good quality—but had seen better days. His clever, delicate hands moved continuously, wavering over the three thimbles, moving first one and then another.

"Come and try your luck, friend," he said in greeting as Davy pushed forward. "Five dollars for the man who can find the pea at the first attempt."

Davy acted as though he was simple-minded, and Jake, watching intently from the bridge, nudged the captain and muttered, "Don't miss this. Friend Davy's up to somethin'."

"What do I have to do?" asked Davy, innocently.

"Simply put down five dollars to match mine, then tell me which of the three thimbles has the pea under it. If you're right you pick up your money and mine as well."

"Sounds easy," said Davy. "But five dollars is a lot o' money to a poor hunter like me."

"Make the stake a dollar then," said the gambler generously.

Davy fished in his pocket for a silver dollar, regarded it doubtfully for a while, and then, as though making up his mind, placed it on the packing case beside the gambler's stake.

"Good," said the gambler. "Now take the pea and put it under whichever thimble you like."

Davy hesitated, then reached forward and slipped the centre thimble over the pea. He stood back and watched carefully as the thimbles were moved this way and that by the smiling man. He followed the progress of his thimble, first to the right, then left, then back into the centre, until he began to feel dizzy. At last the gambler stopped changing the positions of the three little metal cones.

"Which one has got the pea under it now?" he asked.

"Still the middle one," said Davy confidently.

The gambler's hands flashed down, lifted the thimble, and there was the pea. "Very good, friend," he complimented the hunter, handing over his own dollar. "You must have eyes like a hawk. Will you have another try?"

"Reckon so," said Davy, beaming with pretended pleasure. He knew quite well that the gambler had let him win the first game, purely to encourage him.

"Shall we keep the stake the same, or double it?" the rascal asked.

"Make it five dollars this time," Davy suggested.

" Five dollars it is."

Again the process of selecting a thimble, and the involved interchanging of positions went on—only this time the movements were much faster, and Davy had to keep his eyes very alert to follow. Nevertheless he was certain which was the correct thimble when the time came to name it.

The gambler flicked his long fingers down and whipped up the thimble. There was nothing under it.

" Sorry friend," he commiserated, scooping up the hunter's five dollars.

" I'll have another go," said Davy. " Only this time make it ten dollars."

The gambler smiled to himself. He had visions of a very nice profit from the down-river trip if he could find a few more simple people like this man from the backwoods. Obligingly he doubled his stake.

But this time Davy waited until the twirling hands came to rest and the gambler's eyebrows arched inquiringly, inviting him to take his pick. Then he acted. Steel flashed in the sunlight as his hunting knife was plucked from its sheath and held protectively over the thimbles.

" *I'll* do the liftin' mister," he drawled. " Your fingers move a sight too craftily for me."

He raised the left-hand thimble, disclosed the pea it covered, and with a sweep of his palm collected the money from under the gambler's nose.

A pained expression crossed the other's face. " You're not insinuating I would do anything dishonest, are you?" he asked innocently.

"No," said Davy bluntly, as he pocketed the coins "Just makin' sure you don't get a chance!"

The men who watched the play laughed, and began to drift away, deterred from trying their luck by Davy's words. The hunter sheathed his knife and grinned at the gambler, who frowned at him, vexed at his loss of customers.

"This is no way for a man to make his livin'," Davy said scornfully.

The gambler spread his hands wide, expressively. "It's the only way I know," he answered. "You fooled me, stranger. Who are you?"

"David Crockett. What's your name?"

"They call me Thimblerig, or just plain Thimble," said the gambler. "I live by my wits—and I don't get very fat on them. You've cost me a lot of money by casting doubts on my honesty."

"Too bad," said Davy dryly. "But I'd like to know how you make that pea disappear."

Thimblerig grinned. "That's a trade secret," he said, twirling his waxed moustaches. "The quickness of the hand deceives the eye."

They got to their feet and strolled together down the bleached planks of the deck. Davy liked the man in spite of his occupation, and the gambler appeared to bear no ill will over his discomfiture. They chatted amicably of places they had been to, and people they both knew as the river-boat cruised majestically down the Mississippi towards the mouth of the Arkansas.

"Where are you travelling to, Colonel?" Thimblerig asked at length.

"Texas," Davy told him. "Why don't you join us, an' make a new life out there?"

Thimblerig shook his head. "I'm too old a dog to learn new tricks," he said honestly. "The hardest work I've ever done has been shuffling a pack of cards. What would there be for me in Texas?"

Davy laughed. "You could try teaching the Mexicans to play 'Rig the Thimble,'" he suggested, jokingly.

But Thimblerig, always with an eye to business, took him seriously. "You might be right, Colonel," he said thoughtfully, "competition is getting very keen on the river-boats these days."

CHAPTER XIV

Shooting Match at Little Rock

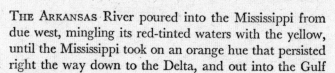

THE ARKANSAS River poured into the Mississippi from due west, mingling its red-tinted waters with the yellow, until the Mississippi took on an orange hue that persisted right the way down to the Delta, and out into the Gulf of Mexico.

It was a treacherous river, in spite of its great width. It twisted and turned this way and that, eating into the rich red soil that formed its banks. As it altered course the currents and eddies threw up vast sand-bars and mud-flats, blocking the channel, and forcing the fast flowing water into new outlets.

The great paddle boat swung out in a wide arc, broadside to the flow of the Mississippi, and nosed its way cautiously into the mouth of the western river. The captain stood close to his helmsman, ready to give instant orders for a change of course should the linesman, poised in the bows, give warning of a hidden sand-bank.

So they steamed westwards, until, some fourteen days after leaving Mill's Point, the township of Little Rock hove in sight ahead on the southern bank.

Davy and Jake took reluctant farewell of the captain,

and passed down the gang-plank to the roughly fashioned jetty. They found the township in holiday mood, for the coming of the steamer was a long-awaited event. Gigs and traps stood wheel to wheel with heavy wagons, while strings of pack horses and mules waited patiently for goods to be transferred from ship to shore.

On the right of the jetty neatly parcelled bales of skins and furs, sacks of grain, and other products of the fertile lands of Arkansas were stacked for shipment. Little Rock was a flourishing settlement, despite the outward appearance of its ramshackle wooden buildings, and the smallness of its population.

The two hunters made for the tavern, and ordered a meal. While they waited they heard a familiar voice raised high above the chatter and laughter of the jostling crowd who filled the building.

" Five dollars for the man who finds the pea !"

" Friend Thimblerig doesn't waste much time !" Davy chuckled, winking at Jake.

" That feller would talk the hind-legs off a chipmunk," said Jake admiringly. " You ought to have had him with you in Congress. You could have run the Government between you an' never given Old Hickory Face Jackson a chance to speak."

At that moment Thimblerig looked up and caught sight of them. He waved cheerily, finished the game he was playing, and got to his feet.

" That's all for now, friends," he told the men around him, " but I'll be back shortly."

He stepped across the room and joined the hunters.

" Top o' the morning to you, Colonel," he said, doffing his silk hat with an extravagant gesture. " I looked for you at the jetty, but I must have missed you." He turned to the landlord, throwing part of his winnings on to a table top. "Bring a tankard of ale for my friend Colonel Crockett," he ordered.

"Davy Crockett! Of course!" the landlord exclaimed. "Since the moment you came in, I've been trying to remember where I'd seen that face before."

Davy turned, a smile of recognition lighting up his eyes with pleasure. Before him stood the sergeant who had faced him on the day the volunteers defied General Jackson at Ten Islands on the Coosa!

"I shan't forget your face as long as I live," grinned Davy. "Never was so frightened in my life! I felt sure you were goin' to pull that trigger."

He took the ex-sergeant's hand and pumped his hand vigorously. Thimblerig looked peeved, his order and even his presence forgotten.

"What are you doing down in Little Rock, Davy?" asked the landlord eventually.

"Goin' to have a look at Texas."

"What for?"

"They tell me it's a rich country, with just about all a man could ask for," said Davy.

"Pah!" the landlord exclaimed. "There's nothin' to beat the State of Arkansas. We've got everything here. The biggest and the fattest bears in America, the richest farming land, the tallest trees, the widest rivers—there's not a thing we haven't got more of than any State in the Union!"

"Sounds quite a country," said Jake dryly.

"Don't take my word for it," protested the landlord.

He turned to the corner of the room, where a group of men lounged against the walls. "Tom! Joshua! Come over here and meet the famous Colonel Crockett. He knows more about Indian fighting than General Jackson and all his officers put together."

Two men detached themselves from the group and came to shake Davy's hand, while the other occupants of the room turned to stare.

"Hear you're quite a marksman, Colonel," stated one of the men. His tone was not particularly friendly. There was a suggestion of condescension in his manner.

"None better in the State o' Tennessee," Jake butted in.

"Is that so?" Again came that slightly sneering tone, and both Davy and Jake felt a challenge in his voice.

"Seen him trim the wick of a candle at thirty paces," went on Jake. "An' he can nick a silver dollar five times out o' six."

"We reckon we're pretty good with a rifle in Arkansas," commented the second man. "Joshua here is our local champion."

"Is that so?" said Davy, mimicking the voice and intonation of the champion. He saw the man flush slightly, and smiled to himself at the sight, thinking how easy it was to rile a conceited man.

"Perhaps the famous Colonel would care to compete in a little friendly shooting match?" asked the champion. "Or maybe he reserves his exhibitions of skill for Tennessee folk?"

This time it was Davy who was annoyed. The man's voice was definitely insulting now.

"Long Betsy an' I will be pleased to give you a lesson any time you like, stranger," he said curtly. "Name the time an' we'll both be there."

"Four o'clock to-morrow afternoon," the champion snarled, and turning on his heel stalked out of the tavern.

*   *   *

Word of the challenge flew round the township and the surrounding country, and by four o'clock on the following day the clearing behind the tavern was thronged with people determined not to miss the fun.

"How are you feelin', Davy?" asked Jake Marshall anxiously.

"Cool as a melon," said Davy. "How d'you expect me to feel? Stop fussin' about like an old hen, Jake, you make me nervous."

"But you're out o' practice, Davy," protested the old hunter. "You've hardly fired a shot in years, what with these Congressman capers you've been gettin' up to, an' one thing an' another."

Davy roared with laughter. "You're an old fool, Jake. You know as well as I do it'd take a better man than this bantam cock of a local champion to lick me. Why, I was winnin' the beef at the matches back home when I was only sixteen! Besides—Long Betsy won't let me down."

But Jake refused to be reassured. He was very proud of his friend's reputation, and genuinely worried that it should hinge on an unasked-for, and unexpected challenge. "Shouldn't never have agreed to it," he muttered to himself as he watched the targets being nailed to a tree at fifty paces.

Presently all was ready. The two men tossed a coin to decide who fired first, and Davy won.

"Let's see what you can do," he told his rival.

"Suits me," came the reply, as the champion took up his position and drew a bead on the target.

"Crack!"

The bullet flew straight as a die. It struck the black circle of the bull's eye, and lodged there, a little high, and a shade to the right of centre.

"Nice shot," said Davy, moving to take his stance. He raised Long Betsy to his shoulder in one graceful movement, took calm, deliberate aim, and squeezed the trigger. As the smoke cleared he saw his bullet had struck the mark within an inch of his rival's. They had both scored bulls.

They fired three shots each at the first target, and when they had finished it was plain there was little to choose between the two marksmen. They were both good. Very good.

A second target was nailed up—at seventy-five paces this time. They fired a further three shots each, and again their scores were equal.

At a hundred paces a target was provided for each man. At this range the long barrelled muzzle-loaders were nothing like as accurate—despite the legends that had been built up around their use by the best marksmen of three continents. But although the margin of error was greater, it was still difficult to find any significant difference between the two men's shots. All the bullets lay within a four inch circle. It looked as though the match would reach stalemate, with the result a draw.

"Let's have two more shots each," suggested Davy.

"Then call it a day. You're a mighty fine shot, Mister."

"You're pretty good yourself," admitted his rival grudgingly.

This time they tossed again to see who fired first, and Davy lost.

"Fire alternately," ordered the judges. "Crockett first. We'll check the targets after you've fired your two shots each."

Like nearly all marksmen of repute, Davy knew instinctively whether his shots were true—although it wasn't possible to see the final position of the bullet at that range. It was an instinct, a feeling, and it rarely let him down. As he pressed the trigger he knew that he had scored another bull. He watched the expression on his rival's face as he took his turn and he was equally certain that he also had scored well.

Davy tipped a measure of powder down the barrel of Long Betsy, rammed home the wad and the leaden bullet, and addressed the target for his final shot.

Almost as he squeezed the trigger his instinct told him the shot was wide. He was certain of it.

His rival took his time reloading, but when he did at last fire he did so confidently, and easily.

Davy was sure he had lost the match.

The judges raced to the targets, and a moment later Davy's fears were confirmed. His second bullet had missed the target completely!

With two bull's eyes to his credit the local champion beamed triumphantly. Davy stepped towards him, his hand outstretched to offer congratulations, when a shout from Jake, who had joined the judges, stopped him in his tracks.

"Missed the target, my foot!" stormed the old hunter. "You people ain't used to real shootin'. Come an' look at this target, an' if you don't agree it's the prettiest piece o' shootin' you've ever seen I'll . . . I'll . . . why, I'll believe every durned thing you tell me about Arkansas!"

The judges and the two contestants crowded around the target. Jake pointed to the one hole that showed clearly in the soft wood of the bull's eye.

"Where's the other bullet, then?" they all asked, puzzled at his words.

"Why here! Look. The second bullet went slap bang on top o' the first one! The two bullets used the same hole!"

"Nonsense!" exclaimed one of the judges. "You don't expect anyone but a fool to believe that, do you?"

"Fool or not, I'd expect a man to believe his own eyes," said Jake scornfully. "Take a good look while I show you the two bullets." He fished in the hole with the tip of his hunting knife, withdrew the bullet, then felt about inside the hole a second time. A moment later another bullet emerged from the hole!

"Now tell me you don't believe me," said Jake expressively.

CHAPTER XV

The Banquet

―――――◁≫≻▷―――――

"Man alive!" cried one of the judges. "This calls for a celebration. We're not likely to see the equal in a lifetime."

"Luckiest shot I ever made," said Davy with a puzzled frown. "Fact is, I could've sworn that bullet was right off the mark."

"You're too modest, Colonel. To-day's match will go down in the history o' Little Rock. It's a great honour to have you here and we only hope you'll stay and hunt with us."

"Nothing I'd like better," Davy replied. "But I'm aimin' to leave in the mornin'—we've got a long way to go, an' a lot o' territory to see."

"More's the pity, Colonel. But come now, we're wasting time. Our friend the landlord has prepared a great feast in your honour. We may not be able to show you how to shoot, but no man can say the folk o' Arkansas don't know how to entertain a guest."

The whole party trooped back to the tavern to find a gigantic meal awaiting them. The massive oak table lay groaning under the weight of great platters of meat, steaming bowls of vegetables, and baskets of fruit. The landlord had excelled himself. There was a haunch of venison at one end, straight from the oven and cooked to a turn. In the centre stood an enormous bear ham, and close to it lay a golden brown turkey-cock that must have weighed all of forty pounds. Foaming tankards of ale stood by every plate, and bottles of wine filled the few spaces that remained on the table. It was a banquet fit for a king.

They seated Davy in the place of honour at the head of the table, among the leading citizens of the township. The landlord welcomed him with a smile.

"I always swore I'd repay that meal you gave us at Ten Islands, Davy," he grinned, briskly stropping a huge carving knife on a steel. "Set to, and if there's any food left over when you've finished I'll want to know the reason why."

Conversation died as the men of Little Rock and their guests attacked the food with a will. Out of the corner of his eye Davy saw Jake Marshall slicing happily at the turkey with his hunting knife, scorning the silver ware that had been brought out for the occasion. Next moment he saw the old hunter reach out for the venison and chop great hunks of meat from it with a flourish. He speared the pieces and crammed them into his mouth while his eyes regarded the bowls and plates about him— fearful lest he should be missing anything.

Presently the wine began to flow, tongues were loosened, and toasts were drunk—toasts to Colonel Crockett, toasts to the landlord, to Little Rock and Tennessee, to the Government of the United States, and to the Frontier. As the serving-maids removed the debris of the meal and the port passed round the table, cries came from all sides demanding a speech from the Colonel.

Davy, mellow and content in this friendly atmosphere, rose to his feet and gave the speech of his life. He told them tales from the woods of Tennessee, tall hunting stories that no one believed but all enjoyed. He talked of politics and of his work in Congress, of the eastern cities he had visited, and of his faith in the future of the Union. He brought forth howls of laughter with his humour and his anecdotes, and spoke to a hushed and attentive audience as he told of Indian fighting days. He held them spellbound by his oratory.

"To-day has been one of the happiest o' days," he ended with sincerity. "The generosity of this feast alone would gladden any man's heart. The landlord has reminded me of the day I stole enough food to feed an army, but Jake Marshall here, and I, can remember long days, and plenty o' them, when we starved with the southern army down at Pensacola. We feasted when we had the luck to shoot a squirrel, an' we were thankful when we could find a snake or a fat lizard to put in the stew pot. We traded powder an' shot for a capful o' corn, an' we slaughtered the Major's horse to make broth for the sick an' wounded.

"A man has a right to live an' a right to eat. He has a right to farm land to feed his family, without the constant fear of war and the threat o' dispossession. That's why we ride for Texas in the mornin'. We go to help the settlers who live in the shadow o' Mexican greed. We'll fight if we have to, for right is on our side an' our dander's up. Long live America—an' to blazes with Mexico!"

A roar of approval greeted Davy's words as he sat down. They slapped his back and shouted for more. But Davy had had his say, and was content.

*   *   *

Next morning the people of Little Rock turned out in force to see Davy and Jake off on the next stage of their journey. They brought two fine horses with them, and refused to accept payment for their use.

"Leave them with our friends in Fulton settlement," they said when Davy protested at their generosity. "They'll see that they are returned to us."

As the two hunters prepared to mount and take their leave, they were amazed to see the elegant, dandified figure of Thimblerig appear round the corner of the tavern, mounted on a Spanish mule. He had a pack strapped to his saddle, a powder horn at his hip, and a long flintlock slung over his shoulder. His tall silk hat still sat incongruously on his carefully waved hair.

"What in the name of all that's wonderful are you doin' in that outfit?" asked Davy, struggling hard to conceal his amusement.

"I'm coming with you, Colonel," Thimblerig announced, as though it were the most natural thing in the world that a man in a frock-coat and fancy waistcoat should join them on their journey across wild and unmapped territory.

"What d'you think, Jake?" Davy asked. "Shall we take him with us?"

"Let him come if he wants to," growled his companion. "We can always eat him if we run short o' food!"

They mounted, called their thanks to the landlord and were beginning to move out of the township when fifty men rode to join them.

"Thought we'd ride with you, Colonel," grinned the leader. "A little company shortens a journey, and the folks would like to be sure you took the right road."

Their hearts warmed by this display of kindness, Davy and Jake stammered their thanks once more, and cantered out of Little Rock to the cheers of the townsfolk.

Their companions led them south-west, on to the faintly marked trail that led in the directon of the Red River. They rode easily, taking time to study the country and listen to tales and legends of the district as they rode. The peaks and crags of the Ozarks showed against the pale winter sky to the north, while southwards stretched low, rolling plains and thick belts of woodland. The trail they followed crossed the foothills of higher country, and was densely wooded throughout. Trees of cottonwood and sassafras crowded each other on all sides, breaking the force of the biting east wind.

They stopped at noon, glad of the warmth of a fire after several hours in the saddle, and soon juicy ribs of meat were roasting on a spit over the glowing embers. They fed well, passing a jug of grog from hand to hand to wash down the meat and the fresh baked bread the landlord had insisted that they took. Eventually the leader of the men from Little Rock rose to his feet.

"We'll have to leave you here, Colonel," he told Davy. "Our wives expect us back by nightfall, and there's quite a way to travel. Take the southern fork where the trail divides, and it'll lead you straight to Red River."

"How far will it be from here?" asked Davy.

"'Bout a hundred and twenty miles, I should reckon. You'll find plenty of sheltered country in which to make camp."

"Good. We're mighty sorry to see you go, an' it'll be a sad day if we should ever forget the kindness you have shown us." Davy took each man's hand in his and shook it warmly.

The three travellers stood by the dying fire and watched the party ride back along the trail. The horsemen paused at the brow of a hill, waved once, and were gone from sight. "Good luck, Colonel!" The words drifted back to them, and all three men suddenly felt they had lost old friends.

They were silent as they gathered their packs and saddled up once more. They doused the fire and rode off into the sinking sun, engrossed in their own thoughts.

It was the irrepressible Thimblerig who broke the silence. He had grown so used to his own company in the solitary life he led, that loneliness was unknown to him. He chattered away, telling Davy and Jake the story of his life, with colourful exaggerations and descriptions that soon had the two men back in their normal high spirits.

"What made you into a gambler, Thimbles?" asked Jake as they rode side by side down the trail.

Thimblerig shrugged. "Just drifted into it I suppose," he said nonchalantly. "I started as an actor on the stage in New Orleans, but I was so bad they threw eggs at me and ruined the only decent clothes I had in the world. I turned to cards for a living, and then to dice, but they caught me cheating and threw me out of town. So then I practised with my thimbles and worked the river-boats. There are worse ways of earning a living."

"Not many," laughed Davy, adding seriously, "You're not as bad as you paint yourself. What made you come with us to Texas?"

For once Thimblerig was stumped for words. "I don't really know, Colonel," he said at length. "Perhaps I felt I would be doing something useful for a change, or perhaps I was swayed by your speech last night. It might have been either of those two reasons, or it may be that I was just bored with riding on the river-boats—who knows?"

"Well, Thimbles," growled Jake, "this trip will more than likely turn out to be the biggest gamble you ever made in your life. Friend Davy here ain't happy unless there's trouble to be found—an' we're headin' right for it if you ask me."

CHAPTER XVI

Crockett's Company

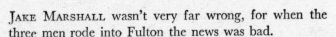

JAKE MARSHALL wasn't very far wrong, for when the three men rode into Fulton the news was bad.

"There's talk of a big Mexican army being formed under General Santa Anna to drive north an' scatter the Texan volunteers," a stranger told them when they asked for news. "If I were you," he added, "I'd keep well away from what don't concern anyone but the Texans. Let 'em fight their own battles, I say."

"You talk like a yellow coward," retorted Davy. "What happens in Texas is the concern o' every man-jack in America."

"Call me names if you like, stranger," went on the man, unperturbed by Davy's words, "but that's what we all think in these parts. We've got worries of our own to attend to without gallivantin' around in strange country pokin' our noses into things that don't concern us."

They found the same reaction everywhere they went. Farms were flourishing, business prospered, and the people were content. They wanted no part in the fighting that all knew was about to break out with the Mexicans. Davy was disgusted. He tried vainly to stir up public feeling and form a company of volunteers to go to the aid of the Texan settlers—but there was no response. He pleaded, he threatened and he cajoled—all in vain.

"It's no good, fellers," he said to Jake and Thimblerig. "They just ain't interested in what happens over the garden fence. This is the richest country I've ever seen. The farmers make a living without trying. The storekeepers can sell everything they can lay their hands on, and the hunters don't have to hunt—the game is so plentiful they only have to walk into the woods an' take what comes along. The country's fat, an' the people are lazy. Let's get out o' here an' find some men o' real grit."

"I'm with you, Davy," grunted Jake. "If we don't go soon I'll find myself settlin' down—an' that would never do. I'd rather die than do that."

"You probably will very shortly," grinned Thimblerig.

"Suits me," Jake answer equably. "Only thing that worries me is what St. Peter will say at the gates o' Heaven when I tell him I've been mixin' with the likes o' you!"

In spite of their friendly bickering they all agreed to press on for the heart of Texas, whether they could find companions to go with them or not. They handed their horses over to a trader who promised to return them safely to their owners in Little Rock, and took passage on the wheezing, diminutive steamer that sailed from Fulton to Natchitoches—on the borders of Louisiana and Texas.

Here the reception was the same, and their stay was brief. They purchased horses to carry them for the rest of their journey, and hurried on towards the sister town-ship of Nacodoches, a hundred miles due west.

Jake sensed the old restlessness returning to his friend. Dave had grown quieter in the last few days. He seemed preoccupied and irritable at even the smallest delay. He still smiled and laughed at the idle bickering that flowed continuously between the old hunter and Thimblerig, but his smile was an absent-minded reaction to the words and phrases—as though he was only half conscious of what went on around him. At times he lapsed into long spells of silence, his thoughts miles away, and then he appeared completely oblivious to the very presence of his companions.

Jake knew the signs of old. "Friend Davy's like an old warhorse," he chuckled to the gambler one night as they made camp and Davy slipped into the brush to hunt their supper.

"He's smellin' trouble, but he don't recognise the smell. You watch him when he starts to follow the scent an' realises what it is. He'll lift up his head and neigh like a stallion, bay like a hound dog, an' bristle like a porcupine!"

They didn't have long to wait. Within days they found themselves high up on the ridge of hills that ringed the border town. They reined to a halt and looked down at the collection of low, single-storied wooden buildings that clustered close together on either side of the one main thoroughfare. They were typical Texan dwellings —the first they had seen. Wide verandas jutted out from the eaves of the shingle roofs, designed to break the merciless glare of the blazing summer sun. Stout poles supported the verandas and served as hitching posts for the many horses and mustangs that waited patiently for their masters as they did business in the stores, or yarned together in the taverns.

From their vantage point the three travellers saw the Republican flag flapping bravely against the tall pole that bore it, and below were grouped men and women listening to political speeches and exhortations from their leaders. The spirit of independence was abroad in Nacodoches.

Davy brightened visibly as they rode down the trail into the township. The slight stoop disappeared from his back, his shoulders squared perceptibly, and the old devil-may-care gleam sprang back into his eyes. Even Thimblerig reacted favourably to the sense of excitement and expectation that filled the air.

Word of their presence in the territory, and of their intended expedition, had preceded them. They were sighted when only half-way down the slope, and within minutes every man and woman in sight flocked up the trail to greet them. A cheer went up as Davy raised his tall figure in his stirrups and waved Long Betsy high above his head.

"Can't say how glad we are to see you, Colonel!" exclaimed one of the men as they approached. "We badly need men o' your calibre to advise us, an' lead us if need be."

"What news o' the Mexicans?" Davy asked, brushing aside the compliments and getting down to brass tacks straight away.

"Bad news," came the reply. "But come and meet our leaders, an' let them give you all the details."

Davy, Jake and Thimblerig found themselves hustled

forward until they reached a big, wide-fronted building. Here they found the elders of the town gathered, and were made welcome to join the discussion that was in progress.

A dignified, white-haired man acted as spokesman. Dressed in a black cut-away coat, white linen shirt and string tie, he looked like a preacher—but was, they learned later, the local surgeon.

" I won't waste words, Colonel Crockett," he started. " You come at an opportune time, for couriers have only recently arrived from Goliad and Bexar. There seems no doubt that Santa Anna is massing a large force to subdue our fellow settlers in southern Texas. Some say his strength is as much as two thousand men—and more are mustering."

" What forces have we at our command?" Davy broke in.

The old man gestured helplessly. " Who knows?" he asked. " Since the Texans seized St. Antonio de Bexar last year to protect the approaches to the territory the army has scattered. A hundred or more are based on Goliad, a mere handful remain at Gonzales, and Colonel Bowie has but one hundred and fifty men at most at Bexar."

Davy whistled expressively. " What's being done to raise more men?" he demanded.

" Precious little. The rumours are so wild and inaccurate that many of the settlers have ceased to believe that they are in danger. Others have fled the country, leaving their farms and cattle behind. Sam Houston is trying to form an army—but by the time he can muster sufficient force it may well be too late."

"Then the sooner we can get to Bowie's aid the better,"
Davy said decisively. "Pass word that I am calling for
volunteers to move within two days, and muster as many
men as you can lay hands on to follow."

*   *   *

A young man stepped from the crowd as Davy and his
companions left the meeting house.

"If you want a guide to show you the trails across the
plains, Colonel, I'll be pleased to be of service. I know
the territory between Nacodoches and Bexar as well as
I know the palm of my hand."

"Good man!" Davy cried, clapping the volunteer
across his broad shoulders. "Get hold o' the best horse
you can find, plenty o' powder an' shot, an' report to me
at the tavern by to-morrow night."

But the good start to the mustering was not continued.
By the time Davy was ready to leave no more than
twenty men had gathered in the yard of the tavern.
Twice as many had vowed they would follow later,
pleading time to settle their affairs and arrange for the
care of their womenfolk. With his meagre force Davy
had to be content.

They rode out of Nacodoches to the cheers of the
townsfolk, the rattle of an ancient drum, and the salute
of a cannon mounted in the square. Their young guide
led them at a brisk pace, their horses climbing steadily
to surmount the ridge. They wheeled westwards as they
reached the top, cut through the tall stand of timber, and
headed for the open prairie.

"How is it that you know the country so well?" asked

Davy of the young man who rode by his side at the head of the column.

"My work takes me to all parts o' the territory," he was told.

"What work is that?"

"I'm what they call a bee-hunter in these parts. I seek out the nests o' wild bees, an' take the wax for candle-making. Sometimes I sell the honey too—but often there is so much that I have to leave it for want o' help to carry it."

"How do you find the nests?" Davy asked, intrigued at hearing of this unusual occupation.

The bee-hunter smiled. "Believe it or not, Colonel," he replied, "I have to stalk every bee I come across! When they're full o' honey they always fly back to the nest or hive in a straight line. If I can pick up the trail, they lead me straight to the very spot I'm searching for."

"You're as bad as Davy when he scents a bear," growled Jake's voice from close behind them. "He takes one look at the tracks, an' before you know what he's up to he's disappeared in a cloud o' dust. An' as for Thimbles here, well, he acts much the same when he hears the clink o' silver coins!"

"That's a thing of the past, Jake," protested Thimble-rig. "I am now a reformed character. No more gambling and evil ways for me. I have left all that behind for good."

"I'll believe that when I see it," grunted Jake.

They rode on steadily, the horses making good progress on the close turf of early spring. They talked and laughed as they rode, getting to know their new companions, and learning something of the terrain through

which they passed. This was the first sight Davy and his
friends had caught of the rolling prairie lands of which
they had heard so much. They thrilled to the sight of
great herds of wild mustangs that roamed at will over
the uplands to the north. Deer grazed undisturbed
around them, and flights of wild game birds passed over-
head with a sighing of wings beating rhythmically on the
still air.

It was different country from any they had known
before. The wild lands of Tennessee and Arkansas were
heavily wooded and split by winding creeks and rivers.
A hunter could travel through the mighty forests for days
without once coming upon a clearing of any size. But
here, in Texas, the vast expanse of the wide open spaces
took their breath away. Even a small hillock gave them
as good a view of the terrain as did a high mountain back
home. For mile upon mile the grasslands stretched,
broken only occasionally by clumps of trees and slow-
flowing streams.

It was on the second day that they spied two forms
ahead of them, making slowly down the trail to the west.
As they drew closer they could make out that one of the
walking men was lean and wiry, dressed in buckskin,
while the other presented an altogether strange picture.
He was short and fat, and walked with the rolling gait
of a sailor. His head was covered by a bright blue necker-
chief, tied at the back of his neck in such a manner that
the surplus material flowed down behind him like a
Chinaman's pigtail. A massive black beard covered
more than half his face and touched his chest which was
clothed in a tight-sleeved waist-length jacket that bore
bold brass buttons. Across his stout back was slung an

ancient flintlock, and hanging by his side, threatening to become entangled with his legs at every step, swung a wide-bladed cutlass.

Davy was about to ask the bee-hunter what he made of the strangers when the young man, shading his eyes to get a better view, gave a cry of pleasure as though he recognised the men.

"Who are they?" Davy asked.

"One's an Indian who wears white man's clothes, and has long forgotten what tribe he belongs to."

"An' the other?"

The bee-hunter laughed. "Why, Colonel, he's a pirate!" he answered. "A laughing, cut-throat rogue of a pirate!"

CHAPTER XVII

The Cougar

"A PIRATE?" echoed Davy.

"Yes, Colonel. He used to sail as bo'sun to Pierre Lafitte, the terror o' the Gulf o' Mexico. He makes a bad enemy, but a warm-hearted friend. I know him well—but no one has ever learned his name."

By this time the horsemen had caught up with the two who trudged along on foot.

"Greetings, friends," called the bee-hunter as they drew level and the men stepped aside to let them pass. "Where are you headed?"

The pirate looked up, recognising the young man's voice. "Well, clap me in irons, if it ain't little Neddy!" he cried in a deep bass voice that bore the unmistakable brogue of Ireland in its notes. "Sure an' it does me heart good to see your smilin' face again. 'Tis to Bexar that we travel. There's fightin' to be had for the asking, so they tell me, an' what could be better than that may I ask?"

"You an' your friend must ride with us," Davy invited. "We have spare horses, and we too go to join Colonel Bowie at Bexar."

The pirate's eyes lit up with pleasure at his unexpected

luck. "Thank you kindly, stranger," he cried. "But you'll have to hoist me aboard an' see me settled all ship-shape an' well secured."

"We'll do that," said Davy with a grin, gesturing for the spare saddle-horses to be led forward. The pirate grasped the thick mane of his horse as high as he could reach, and shook with laughter as two of the riders took him firmly by the legs and heaved him up on to the animal's bare back. The Indian, who had not spoken a word, mounted the mustang that was led forward for his use with easy grace, nodding his thanks with unsmiling dignity.

"Cast off, me hearties!" roared the pirate, and with a slap from the flat of his cutlass he urged his mount ahead, to the cheers of the volunteers.

They rode hard all that day and the next, stopping briefly for a meal at noon, and camping in what shelter they could find in the lee of the gentle slopes. Davy's impatience was more evident than ever. He drove his men to the limit, brushing aside their grumbles and insisting that they broke camp at first light.

They were brewing coffee over a fire of buffalo chips at a midday halt, when Jake Marshall cocked an ear to the north, and listened intently.

"Quiet a minute," he called, and as his companions stopped their chatter they plainly heard the drumming of a thousand hooves over the prairie.

Davy raced to the brow of a small hillock and stared out in wonder at the sight that lay before him.

An enormous herd of animals sped towards them, seeming to fill the whole plain below with the dark brown of their straining bodies. Flying hooves tore into the turf, ripping it into shreds before his eyes.

"Buffalo!" cried one of the men who had stepped up beside him.

"So that's what they are! Ain't never seen those critturs before," Davy shouted back, his words drowned in the thunder of the herd's progress. "Look at that feller in front!"

A massive black bull led the herd in its mad stampede. Head down and bloodshot eyes fixed straight ahead it made directly for the camp. It reached the curve of the hillock, and wheeled suddenly to the right, the packed cows and young bulls swinging in his wake.

Davy grabbed Long Betsy, took careful aim and fired at the leader. They saw the great bull check for an instant as the bullet struck. It shook its massive, shaggy head in anger, but continued at a run with as little worry as though an angry bee had stung it.

Davy was wild at the lack of regard the bull paid to his well-aimed shot. "I'll get you, you black varmint!" he yelled. He sprang for his horse, and without stopping to think, tore off in pursuit of the herd.

He drove his horse unmercifully, urging it to the limit, until the lather formed in long ribbons on its sides. But all the time the herd gained on him. He followed them over first one brow and then another, swinging left and right in their wake as some obstacle barred their passage.

He nearly caught up with them once as they passed through a narrow gully that slowed their speed, but they were through it just in time to prevent him taking a second shot. They put on speed and streamed across the open plain beyond, stretching out until they seemed to merge with the horizon. It was no good. His horse just could not match the buffalo for speed or stamina.

Davy drew rein, and let his horse take a badly needed breather. He sank to the ground himself, glad of a break from the excitement and energy of the chase. He followed the herd regretfully with his eyes until he saw them disappear over the skyline like a big dark cloud.

As the sound of the buffaloes' hoof-beats receded in the distance, a strange silence descended on the prairie. It was as though the sudden passage of the herd had shocked Mother Nature into holding her breath. Even the air took on an unnatural stillness.

Davy felt a wave of dejection steal over him. He was beginning to feel he had made a fool of himself in his mad career after the herd—as in fact he had. He rose to his feet, and walked to his horse. It stood with bowed head, its ribs still heaving as it fought to regain its wind. Davy took the saddle from its back and used the saddle blanket to rub the sweat and lather from the animal's hide. As he did so he looked about, trying to get his bearings.

He looked first in one direction, then another, but the country was featureless. The noonday sun shone high above his head, as though mocking him as it gave no clue to north, south, east or west. Slowly the realisation came to him that he had no idea where he was, nor in which direction lay the camp!

"This won't do," he muttered, as much to the horse as to himself. He replaced the saddle, pulled tight the single cinch, and led the horse up on to higher ground. Again he stared to all points of the compass—but it was no good. He was lost!

For three hours Davy rode over the plain, working from ridge to ridge. Once he thought he saw smoke in the distance. He shook the horse into a gallop and rode hard in that direction. The smoke, if it had been smoke at all, faded from sight, and although he rode the same course for the best part of a further hour he found no fire, no camp, and no evidence of man or beast on the prairie.

At last he gave up. He turned the horse's head towards a small stream that flowed from a spring-fed water-hole, and made camp.

* * *

Davy was tired, hungry, and becoming increasingly annoyed with himself.

"Of all the fool things to do!" he mused. The stream gurgled musically, as though agreeing with him. "Here I am, one o' the finest scouts in the West, an' yet unable to follow my own tracks back to camp!" He spoke out loud to break the monotonous silence.

He pushed his way into a nearby thicket by a fallen tree and gathered dead wood with which to make a fire. He had left his bed-roll and rations behind at the noon-day camp, so there was nothing to cook, but the cheerful blaze warmed him, and he took fresh heart. Soon he found himself laughing at the silliness of his actions. "The great Colonel Crockett behavin' like a tenderfoot," he grinned. "Hope the folks back in Tennessee never hear o' this!"

As night fell and the dew began to form on the grass, he forsook the fire and perched his lanky form between two branches of the fallen tree. Within minutes he was asleep.

It was barely light when he awoke with a start.

He sat up abruptly, the tail-end of a frightened neigh echoing in his ears. Something had scared his horse, and scared it badly if he was any judge. He reached for Long Betsy, and as he did so he heard a noise that froze him motionless.

There was no mistaking that hissing screech. He felt the hair on the back of his neck rising, and his heart beat a crazy tattoo against his ribs. He looked up slowly. A cougar crouched above him, poised among the branches of the same tree that supported him!

For what seemed an eternity Davy stared into the evil green eyes of the great tawny mountain cat. He saw it settle back on its hind feet, preparing to spring. He couldn't move. He sat motionless mesmerised with fear.

Then, abruptly, the spell broke. He flung Long Betsy to his shoulder and fired at point-blank range.

The cougar screamed as the bullet struck, but it was no more than a flesh wound. Davy saw it bunch its body for another spring, and next instant the beast was on him.

He lashed out with the rifle in a furious attempt to ward the cougar off. The rotten wood of the dead tree cracked and split, and they fell to the ground, locked together.

Davy felt an agonising pain as the vicious claws dug into his thighs, tearing through the buckskin leggings and lacerating his flesh. He thrust his left arm up to shield his face from the snarling jaws, and with his right hand he felt frantically for his knife. His groping fingers locked about the hilt. He drew the blade and drove it hard into the wild cat's unprotected belly. He thrust and thrust again, furiously, desperately, as the white teeth bit hard upon his arm. He felt a shudder pass over the animal's body, and with a superhuman effort he brought his legs up, and kicked hard at the writhing form.

The cougar fell away from him, its front claws still hooked in the leather of his jacket. He felt himself dragged off balance, and they both rolled down the sloping bank of the stream, almost to the water's edge. The cougar kicked twice and went limp.

Davy staggered to his feet. He stood looking at the dead beast, swaying unsteadily, trying to focus his eyes. A thick red mist seemed to blot out his vision. He felt his knees buckle, and he fell face downward into the water.

CHAPTER XVIII

Comanche Medicine

————— ❦ —————

THE COLD water stung Davy back into consciousness. His brain cleared and he crawled painfully out of the water-hole. He lay for a while on the bank regaining his strength, then stumbled to the embers of his fire and stirred them into a blaze. He threw on fresh wood and warmed himself.

It was only then that he examined his wounds. He had been severely mauled by the cougar. His leg was badly torn, and the muscle of his left arm had been pierced by the animal's teeth.

He bathed the worst of his injuries and bound them up as best he could. He had been remarkably lucky to escape comparatively lightly—a few days' rest and care would see him fit again.

He limped down to the water's edge and looked at the cougar. "It was you or me, Mr. Cat," he said with feeling, "an' I'm mighty glad it turned out to be you!" He was standing there considering whether he should take the skin and find out what cougar meat tasted like, when the sound of galloping hooves came to his ears. He turned eagerly, expecting to find that his friends had come in search of their leader—but instead he found himself watching the rapid approach of a band of Indian horsemen. He bent swiftly and retrieved Long Betsy from the tangle of broken branches at his feet. He checked the mechanism, found it free and unharmed, and loaded quickly.

"Out o' the fryin' pan into the fire," he muttered to himself as the Indians raced towards him. He saw them fan out to circle the water-hole, hauling hard on the horse-hair bridles to turn their horses. A quick count told him there were thirty braves in the party—mounted bareback on wiry little mustangs similar to his own. Each man carried a bow and a quiver full of arrows, with the exception of the central figure, who wore a head-dress of wild goose feathers instead of the single feather of the braves. Resting across the neck of his mount lay a white man's rifle.

"Well, chief," thought Davy, as the riders came to a halt and sat staring at him in silence, "the first move is yours. An' if I ain't a dead duck after that, then *you* will be." He held Long Betsy ready, and kept his eyes fixed on the chief's face.

Neither the chief's eyes nor his features gave any clue to his thoughts. He met Davy's stare without blinking. He was not a tall man, but there was strength in his deep chest and arms. He held himself proudly, with all the dignity of a Comanche chieftain of the full blood. His braves waited, immobile as statues.

Davy felt the perspiration beading on the palms of his hands. Long Betsy began to feel like a ton weight as the long seconds mounted into minutes. The tension in the air was unbearable.

Suddenly, in one swift, graceful movement, the Comanche chief slid from his horse. He alighted on the turf with only the lightest murmur of sound and stepped forward. Davy's grip on his rifle tightened, his finger flexed about the trigger, but the chief ignored him. He walked right past the white man, without as much as looking at him. Down to the edge of the water he went, pausing only when he reached the body of the cougar.

Davy turned to watch the chief. He saw the Indian roll the beast's body over with his foot, and study the knife wounds in its skin. He exclaimed aloud with a guttural grunt and gestured to his braves to join him.

The Comanches sprang from their mustangs and hurried to the spot. They pawed the carcass, rolling it first this way then that, counting the wounds and jabbering excitedly among themselves as they did so. Davy lowered his rifle to the ground, and leaned upon the muzzle, his presence completely ignored.

Presently the chief came over to him. He smiled into Davy's eyes, then reached forward and patted the hilt of his hunting knife. "Americano brave hunter," he said surprisingly, in recognisable English.

Davy stood open-mouthed with astonishment. "Well, if that don't beat all!" he spluttered, letting loose a peal of laughter. "I thought you were about to scalp me, chief."

"Comanche friend of Americanos," the chief beamed. "Americanos give me gun, teach me how kill buffalo."

As they spoke together the braves were busy skinning the cougar. Within minutes the tawny pelt was stripped from the carcass and expertly rolled, fur innermost. Davy indicated by signs that he had no use for it, for he had just learned from the chief that the Comanches had been hunting the cougar for the best part of two days, following the loss of a valuable horse. It was, in fact, the closeness of the pursuit that had driven the mountain cat from its lair to the north, where the prairie merged with the foothills. Harried by the hunting party, the cougar had taken advantage of the darkness to sneak into open country and make for the security of the tree-lined water-hole.

But the chief had other news for Davy that was of much greater interest. He had seen a party of horsemen scouring the plains to the east, and there was little doubt from his description of the riders that Davy's Company had been located.

" Take me to them," he demanded eagerly, his hunger and even the smarting of his wounds forgotten in his relief.

The chief shook his head. " When hunters meet it is good that they should take food together," he said solemnly. " No friend leaves a Comanche with an empty belly. Later we will take the Americano to his people."

Davy knew it was useless to argue, and as the smell of roasting meat came to his nostrils he realised that it was many hours since he had eaten. He sank to the ground and started to re-tie one of his blood-stained bandages. The chief knelt beside him and bent to examine the wound. He shouted to one of his men and waited for the brave to fetch a deerskin pouch from his horse.

" What're you goin' to do?" Davy asked as the pouch was opened to disclose a thick wad of moss and strange twisted leaves.

" Comanche make you well," the chief grunted in

reply. He took the dried leaves in his long, brown fingers and crushed them into small fragments. Then he sprinkled each wound in turn with the strong-smelling particles, placed a layer of moss on top, and strapped the bandage firmly in place.

Miraculously the pain of the torn flesh eased, and the throbbing died down. "That's powerful medicine, chief!" Davy grinned. "What tree are those leaves from?"

"That is the secret of the Comanches," said the Indian gravely. "Each summer, when the sun is strong and the grasses wither, the squaws of my tribe gather the leaves and store them for our use. So it was in the day of my father, and in the day of my father's father."

As the Comanches gathered round to eat their meat Davy saw their eyes turned to where Long Betsy lay on the grass beside him. He said nothing, but when the meal was over he gave the Indians a display of shooting that brought cries of wonder from all directions. He placed a dollar on a rock and sent it flying with one shot from fifty paces. He took a feather from the head of one of the braves, set it in the ground and snapped it neatly in two. He gave his hat to another man, made him throw it in the air and drilled a hole in it before it hit the ground.

When he had exhausted all his tricks he handed the rifle to the chief, who stroked it lovingly, as though it were a living thing. The Indian shook his head sadly as he picked up his own decrepit weapon and compared the two. Davy smiled.

"Take me to my people, chief," he stated, "an' I'll see you get a good rifle for your trouble."

He kept his word two hours later, when the Comanches

led him to join his friends. The chief reined to a halt
and pointed to a clump of cottonwoods. A thin spiral of
smoke twisted skywards and several horses could be seen
tethered among the trees.

Davy clapped his heels against the flanks of his mustang
and led the whole band of Indians in a gallop towards
the camp. So great was his pleasure at finding his companions that he let out a wild yell that was echoed in a
laughing chorus by the Comanches who rode beside him,
crouched low over the necks of their horses.

" Crack ! "

A shot came from the trees and a bullet whined over
their heads. With a shock Davy realised that he was
being fired on by his own men ! He shouted to the
Indians to halt and rode forward alone. As he approached
the camp he saw the figures of Jake and Thimblerig step
out into the open and he headed for them at a trot.

"You crazy idiots!" he shouted as they recognised
him. "You might've killed me."

Jake ran forward to meet him. " Fine time to play at
Indians!" he grumbled, puffing from his exertions. " We
thought we'd got a battle on our hands." He pointed
behind him, and Davy saw one man after another rise
to his feet from the cover of the trees. Each carried a
rifle, and they all cast anxious glances to where the Comanches had halted.

Davy laughed. " Sorry to worry you, fellers," he
called. " Come an' meet some friends o' mine." He
beckoned to the waiting Indians and saw them ride slowly
towards him.

" Where've you been, Colonel?" asked Thimblerig.
" We've searched the whole prairie for you. We tried to

follow your trail, but those buffalo must've circled back over their own tracks. We found ourselves going round in circles."

Davy nodded. "Same thing happened to me, Thimbles. Never should've found you without the help o' these Comanches."

"What's wrong with your arm an' leg?" asked Jake, eyeing the bandaged wounds. "You been in trouble again?"

"Mosquito bit me," grinned Davy.

"Sure an' 'tis good to see you, Skipper!" roared the pirate, as he joined them. "Thought we'd lost you overboard."

"Not this time," Davy smiled. "But if Jake here grumbles at me any more I reckon I'll go back again."

CHAPTER XIX

The First Mexicans

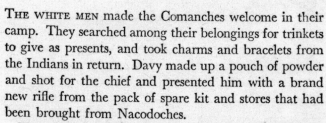

THE WHITE MEN made the Comanches welcome in their camp. They searched among their belongings for trinkets to give as presents, and took charms and bracelets from the Indians in return. Davy made up a pouch of powder and shot for the chief and presented him with a brand new rifle from the pack of spare kit and stores that had been brought from Nacodoches.

The chief unrolled the cougar skin and showed it to Davy's men, proudly pointing to the knife cuts, and then at the tall hunter.

"I suppose you call that a mosquito skin?" growled Jake, winking at his friend.

"Yes, that's right," agreed Davy, grinning broadly.

"Well, in that case I'd hate to be bitten by a Texas horse-fly," said the old man. "Reckon it'd kick me to death while it was bitin'!"

When the Comanches did eventually ride back towards the hills Davy turned to Jake, who was busy saddling his horse.

"There's nothin' better than a good Indian," he said seriously.

Jake scratched the back of his neck thoughtfully for a moment before he replied.

"Maybe you're right, Davy," he said. "But whether it's a good Indian or a bad Indian I'm standin' next to, the effect's the same."

"What d'you mean?"

"The hair on the top o' my head always seems to stand up and wait to be scalped!"

Davy laughed. "They do say that it was a white man who first taught the Indians to scalp, Jake. Jedidiah Smith an' a few more o' the frontiersmen who blazed the trails westwards certainly took scalps when they killed an Indian."

"So I've heard," grunted the old hunter. "But that don't make me feel any easier. Whoever started it makes no difference. The perishin' red men like doin' it a sight too much for me!"

Jake, as usual, had the last word. He snapped his leather girth-strap through the brass buckle, put his foot in the stirrup and heaved himself into the saddle. He waited for Davy to mount, knowing better than to offer help to the wounded leader. He saw his friend wince at the pain from his leg, and noticed the uselessness of the injured left arm, but he said nothing. He had already warned the others to slow their pace when they continued their journey to Bexar. "That's all we can do to help an ornery cuss like Davy," he had told them. "By rights he ought to lay up for a few days, but you won't catch him doin' that. He's just plain stubborn."

*   *   *

It was several days before Davy's wounds healed. If it hadn't been for Jake's orders it would have been considerably longer. Davy fumed and stormed at the slow progress they were making, but his words had no effect. The riders took their pace from Jake and refused to be hurried.

First the bee-hunter pretended that his horse had gone lame. Then Thimblerig deliberately left his rifle behind when they broke camp, and the whole company had to wait for him to catch them up. They pulled every trick they could think of until they were sure that the Colonel's recovery was complete. Then they let him set the pace, and the miles flew by.

It was late one afternoon that they caught sight of the raiders ahead.

" Enemy on the port bow!" shouted the pirate as the figures crossed the skyline.

" You've got good eyes!" Davy exclaimed.

" 'Tis the eyes of a man that are the saving of him when he sails in foreign waters," came the laughing reply.

" What d'you make o' them, pirate?"

" Mexicans by their rig, sor."

" How many?"

" Best part o' thirty, from what I can see. All sails set an' comin' up fast."

Davy didn't hesitate. " Make for that clump o' trees, men," he ordered. " Get the horses under cover, an' prime your rifles. If it's trouble they want they've come to the right place for it!"

The whole party hurried to the lone thicket that sprouted out of a mound of rock and soil several hundred yards away. They took up their positions and watched the approach of the Mexicans. The distance between them closed rapidly, and soon they could clearly see the glint of sword and lance, the dull gleam of gun metal, and the flashing sparkle of the spring sunshine on the ornate gold braid of the cavalry uniforms.

The pirate's estimate of strength had been very accurate. There were thirty-three riders, superbly mounted on black and dun coloured horses that showed unmistakably the lines and bearing of their Arab ancestors. The swarthy, black-haired Mexicans rode with a swagger, the gaily-coloured pennants at the tips of their lances fluttering jauntily in the breeze. They made straight for the waiting Americans, spreading out into a long line as they came. At their centre rode their captain, an elegant, moustachioed man, resplendent in a plumed three-corner hat.

" Dressed like an Admiral," muttered the pirate, scornfully.

" Hold your fire," Davy ordered as the Mexicans came to a halt well within rifle shot. " Let them make the first move, but pick a man each an' be ready to drop him when I give the word." As he spoke the Mexican captain rode forward, stood up in his stirrups and called to them in his own tongue.

" What's he say, pirate?" asked Davy.

The old sailor chuckled. " He says we must surrender or his men will fire an' give us no quarter."

" Does he, by Heaven!" Davy roared. " I'll soon change his tune for him." He put Long Betsy to his shoulder, squinted down the sights and pressed the trigger. His companions saw the plumed hat suddenly whipped from the captain's head as the bullet struck its crown. It hit the ground and rolled over to the feet of the fidgeting horses. A cheer welled up from the thicket, to be answered by a volley of shots from the Mexicans.

The bullets spattered into the trees above their heads, making them duck, but causing no casualties.

"You'll have to do better than that, my beauties," grunted Jake, taking careful aim at a fat sergeant ahead of him. To his left Thimblerig twirled his moustaches with a flourish and settled himself comfortably in the grass under the trees. His tall silk hat lay carefully placed in the shade, removed at the first sign of danger in case it got damaged in the affray. Farther off, the pirate could be seen tucking his long black beard into the neck of his shirt to keep it out of the way of the hammer of his rifle. He sighted quickly and waited for Davy's command.

" Fire !"

Davy's men fired as one. A dense cloud of gun-smoke rose up from the thicket, and as it cleared they saw six riderless horses rearing high in fright. There was consternation in the ranks of the Mexicans. Of the captain there was no sign—Davy had taken care of him. Leaderless, the cavalry men milled around in panic, then streaked off in the direction from which they had come.

"After 'em !" yelled Davy, racing for his horse. His men broke cover, leading their horses. They mounted as soon as they were free from the trees. They spurred hard and tore off after the retreating Mexicans, yelling like a thousand devils in their excitement.

Far out across the open prairie they chased. They rode like drunken Indians—careless of their own comfort or even of the safety of their horses. But the Mexicans had

a head start on them, and their horses were in a class
apart from the broken-winded mustangs of the Americans. Slowly they pulled away, to pass out of range in
their desperate bid for safety from the snap shots that
followed them.

"No sense in killin' our horses," shouted Davy dis-
gustedly when he saw the chase was useless. He eased his
mustang to a trot, then to a walk, and his men slowed
their pace on either side. He ran his eyes over the party
to check for casualties, and with a sudden sick feeling in
the pit of his stomach he noticed that Thimblerig was
missing.

"Where's Thimbles?" he inquired, anxiously. No one
seemed to know.

"He was close behind me when we went to free the
horses," said Jake. "Forgot all about him till now."

They looked back towards the thicket, but there was
no sign of the gambler. There was no need for orders—
with one accord they wheeled their horses and rode fast
for the thicket. They called out as they approached, but
no answering shout came.

"He must've caught a stray bullet," muttered Jake
as they dismounted and pushed their way between the
trees. But the thicket was empty. Neither Thimblerig
nor his horse could be found. They had both disappeared
into thin air.

CHAPTER XX

The Alamo

"IT LOOKS as though his horse bolted," said one of the men, pointing to the broken branch of a shrub, and the trampled earth at the far side of the trees.

"In that case he may be anywhere by now," stated Davy. "A scared horse can travel a good many miles in half an hour, an' no one could call Thimbles an expert horseman."

"What shall we do, Colonel?" asked one of the men.

"There's only one thing to do. Spread out, an' ride to all points o' the compass. But look out for more Mexicans, these parts aren't too healthy. Fire a couple o' shots if you find him, an' meet back here as soon as you can."

The party split up and began to scour the prairie for the missing gambler. Davy and Jake rode east, pausing at every ridge or rise in the ground that they came upon to search the distance.

The day was beginning to fade when a flicker of light caught Davy's eye half a mile to the south. "What's that, Jake?" he called.

"Pah! That's only the sunset reflecting on water," the old hunter scoffed. "Your eyes are playin' you tricks."

"Take another look, Jake. We passed through there this mornin' an' there's no water for miles. That's a fire burnin' beside those rocks."

"Well, there's no use in arguin', Davy. Let's go take a look. We'll soon know who's right."

They hadn't ridden far before they saw that Davy was right. A small fire crackled and spat, burning brightly in the evening dusk. They approached carefully, lest they should be riding straight into a camp of Mexicans or hostile Indians—but they needn't have worried.

Thimblerig sat on a rock before the fire, his city clothes smothered in mud, and his trousers badly torn. In front of him lay his silk hat, crown uppermost, and Davy and Jake saw the glint of metal in the firelight. The incorrigible gambler was playing "Rig the Thimble" with himself!

"Bet he's cheatin' too," chuckled Jake. "That feller's as crooked as a corkscrew."

"Stay here an' watch," whispered Davy, slipping from his horse and making for the cover of the tallest rock. Jake grinned as he followed his friend's progress. He moved silently through the shadows like a disembodied ghost, creeping nearer and nearer to the unsuspecting gambler. Jake saw him stop behind the rock and next instant the spine-chilling screech of a hyena pierced his eardrums.

Thimblerig jumped two feet in the air with fright. He grabbed a blazing pine bough from the fire, and held it protectively in front of him, as though to ward off the attacking beast. His face was the colour of ashes.

"You've got more sense than I credited you with, friend Thimbles," laughed Davy as he stepped out from behind the rock. "You might've saved your skin if it *had* been a cat."

"Why! You . . . you . . . cold-blooded heathen!" cried the gambler. "I thought my last moment had come."

"Sorry Thimbles, but you looked so comfortable sittin' there after we've been scouring the whole territory for you. Thought you deserved a fright."

"Funniest thing I've seen in years!" laughed Jake, leading his horse forward. "But what happened to you? Where's your horse?"

"The ornery crittur bolted and when I tried to curb it the girth-strap snapped. I landed on my back with the saddle on top of me."

"Where's the horse now?" asked Davy.

"Couldn't say, Colonel. I must've passed out, and when I came to, the horse wasn't in sight. I was left with a damaged saddle, a sore back, and a broken rifle." He pointed to the dented barrel and shattered stock of his flintlock. "I'll have to borrow another rifle from you before we get to Bexar," he added, ruefully. "This one is past repairing."

As they spoke Jake and Davy picked up the gambler's saddle and perched it on the back of Davy's horse. They strapped it securely and Davy took his seat behind it. Thimblerig doused his fire and mounted behind Jake, and they moved away from the rock and travelled slowly for the camp.

"Too late to signal now," said Davy when they were half-way to the thicket. "The boys will all be in by now, an' they'll figure we've run across Thimbles. Only hope they've had the sense not to light a fire. We don't want a band o' greasers surprising us during the night."

*   *   *

After a good night's sleep Thimblerig was none the worse for his misfortune, but he had to take a lot of chaffing from his friends. Luckily two of the Mexicans' horses had been captured after the attack, and he found himself mounted on the best of these when they set off for the final stage of their journey.

"Not far to go now," the pirate told them after the noon halt. "When we clear that gully an' come out on the higher ground we'll see San Antonio River below us."

Their first impression of Bexar was of a peaceful Mexican township surrounded by well cultivated fields of rich soil. The river wound through the centre of the town, separating the white adobe buildings from each other. Along its banks grew strong clumps of graceful willows, bobbing their heads to the ever-present breeze of Texas.

Many of the houses were no more than one-room hovels, their entrances merely open archways, and their windows unglazed. Other buildings were more substantial, with columned doorways and overhanging balconies. Most were flat-roofed, and many sported roof gardens of trailing plants and cacti.

A few donkeys and a mule or two were tethered in the shade of the main street, but of people there were none. San Antonio de Bexar was like a city of the dead—deserted and empty. Davy led his men through the silent streets, the hooves of their horses raising an echo from the crowded adobe walls. They stopped to water their horses at the river bank, but although they took their time they saw no movement among the buildings, and their voices fell flatly upon the silence of the town.

"Gives a feller the creeps," said Jake, his voice hushed to a hoarse croak. "The sooner we get to this Alamo place an' find some of our own kind the better I shall like it. Where does it lie?"

"At the far end o' the town," the pirate answered him. "It's that tall-fronted, square building you can just see showin' over the roofs."

"What is it—a fort, or the meeting hall, or just a big house?" asked Thimblerig.

The bee-hunter answered him. "A bit of each, Thimbles. It was built as a church, or mission, by the Spaniards, but the Comanches and the Apaches were raidin' through here all the time so they made it as solid an' secure as they could. They built a granary, an' a storehouse, an' piped water to it, an' surrounded the whole place with thick walls an' a barred doorway. In times o' trouble they herded there an' shut themselves in."

"Sounds quite a place," said Jake.

"It is," the bee-hunter agreed. "Given five hundred men it could be held against an army."

"From what I hear Colonel Bowie's only got a bare hundred an' fifty men—countin' us," said Davy soberly, "so it'd better be as strong as you say, bee-hunter, or our goose is cooked."

They led their horses from the water's edge and rode on towards the Alamo. As they approached they made out the figures of sentries on the battlements above the porch, and saw bearded faces peering at them from the barricaded windows high above the street. A slim fair man stepped into the open and hailed them from between cupped hands.

"Who are you, and what d'you want here?"

Davy rode forward alone. "Colonel Crockett's Company reportin' to Colonel Bowie," he yelled in reply.

The fair man turned and shouted to someone out of sight of the riders. "Throw open those gates, an' give a right royal welcome to Colonel Davy Crockett." He bobbed down below the parapet and a moment later Davy heard the heavy bars across the doorway being withdrawn. With a creaking of rusty hinges and a rattling of chains the massive woodwork swung inwards, and he led his company through the opening—into the Fortress of the Alamo.

CHAPTER XXI

The Three Colonels

—————◦◦◦◦◦—————

A ROUSING cheer greeted Davy and his men as they clattered into the Alamo. Nearby a hundred men had gathered to welcome them, forsaking their posts on the battlements, or interrupting their off-duty chores and pleasures. Friendly hands helped unload the packs and trail kits, and led the horses away for feeding and grooming in the stables.

Davy dismounted and the fair man who had challenged him stepped forward, his hand outstretched in welcome.

"You're a sight for sore eyes, Colonel," he stated warmly. "My name's James Bowie of Louisiana."

"Right glad to meet you, Colonel Bowie," said Davy with genuine pleasure. "There's not a man in the States who hasn't heard o' your exploits an' your famous knife."

Colonel Bowie laughed. He patted the murderous-looking knife that hung in a long buckskin sheath from his belt. "Don't feel dressed without it, Colonel Crockett," he grinned. "I only hope you've brought Long Betsy with you. We can do with her help."

"She's with me," smiled Davy, "an' what's more she's already done a little barkin' at the Mexicans."

"Glad to hear it, Colonel. But come now, I'm forgettin' my manners. You must be fed an' rested. We can talk later."

The commander of the Alamo led Davy and his men into the main building, showed them to their quarters and hustled up the cooks to provide a meal in double-quick time. While they ate Davy talked to Bowie and found out all he could of the nature of the man under whom he was to serve.

James Bowie was slight of build, fair-haired and pink-complexioned. His eyes held a merry twinkle of good humour. He wore the dress of a plainsman—fringed hunting shirt, leather breeches, and Indian moccasins—and he carried himself with a confident swagger. It was plain that he was an able man who didn't know the meaning of fear. The more he saw of him the more Davy liked him.

A slim, dark-featured man walked in to join them as they finished their meal. His thin face and piercing eyes proclaimed a nature as serious as James Bowie's was light-hearted. He walked purposefully towards them, his bearing that of a trained soldier, in spite of his youth. Davy summed him up in three words: efficient, intelligent, and incorruptible. Bowie rose to his feet to introduce them.

"Meet Colonel Barrett Travis of Texas," he said simply.

"Glad to know you, Colonel," Davy acknowledged.

"My apologies for not being at hand to welcome you, Colonel Crockett. I was asleep when you arrived," the newcomer explained. "We have to stand night and day duty at present."

"You'd better let me take over to-night, in that case," Davy offered. "I'm sure you two can do with a relief."

"That's something we'll have to settle straight away," broke in Bowie. "You see, Colonel Crockett, you are the senior Colonel of us three. It is our pleasure to ask you to take over command of the Alamo. Needless to say Colonel Travis and I shall be honoured to serve under so distinguished an officer."

"Seniority be hanged!" Davy burst out. "I came here to help you, not to parade my seniority like a turkey-cock. Call me what you will, I'm fightin' under your command as plain Mr. Davy Crockett!"

"But Colonel! It is your right to take command," protested Travis.

"Right, nonsense," smiled Davy. "This is Texas, not Tennessee. Say no more about it. I'm here to carry out your orders as an ordinary volunteer—just like the rest o' my company."

"As you wish, Colonel," agreed Bowie.

"I do wish it," grinned Davy. "An' stop calling me Colonel all the time. My name's Davy to my friends."

*   *   *

Jake Marshall sat on the edge of his mattress cleaning his rifle when Davy came in from his talk with the two colonels.

"What news?" he inquired, raising one eyebrow and studying his friend's serious face.

"Pretty bad, Jake," said Davy soberly .

"How bad?"

"Santa Anna's on his way all right. Some friendly

Mexicans slipped in to Bexar to report to Bowie that a large army is only a few days' march from here. There's little doubt that Santa Anna plans to lay seige to us. We can expect fireworks any day now."

"Suits me."

"Don't you speak too soon, Jake. There's mighty few of us here, an' between you an' me we don't stand much chance unless reinforcements arrive from Goliad, or points west."

"What are the chances o' that happening?"

"Mighty slim if you ask me, but you never can tell. It all depends on what Santa Anna does."

"How d'you mean, Davy?" Jake looked puzzled. "What difference does it make what that greaser does? If he attacks, then he attacks—an' that's all there is to it."

Davy smiled. "It's not quite as simple as that, Jake," he explained. "Santa Anna may sit here at Bexar with enough men to keep us bottled up, while the rest o' his men attack Goliad. If that happens we shan't get any help at all."

Jake whistled through his teeth. "Now I get you," he said thoughtfully.

"What is the Mexican Army like, Colonel?" asked Thimblerig, who had joined them. "Are they good soldiers?"

Davy shrugged his shoulders. "Some are," he told the gambler, non-committally. "The officers are good, an' some o' the regulars are first-class. The rest are the scum of every jail from here to Mexico City—gutter rabble. The worst of our men are worth ten o' that type."

"What about Santa Anna? What sort o' man is he?"

"From what Bowie tells me he's as cunnin' as a fox, as vain as a peacock, an' as vicious as a wounded hyena."

"Steady, Davy," Jake interrupted. "You'll be givin' poor old Thimbles goose-pimples again if you're not careful."

"I've got them already," said Thimblerig.

Davy got to his feet and moved to the door of the barrack-room.

"Where are you off to?" Jake asked.

"Goin' to meet some o' the boys, an' find out what sort o' men we'll be fightin' with. Comin' along?"

"Be right with you."

The sentries were changing as Davy and Jake walked out on to the battlements to survey the Alamo and its defenders. They introduced themselves and soon Davy had the men laughing at his description of their journey from Little Rock to Bexar. He coloured all his tales and anecdotes with the vividness of his fertile imagination, exaggerating the details and even adding purely fictional incidents. The men warmed to his company and told him much of their own background.

They were of all kinds, and their reasons for being at the Alamo were just as varied. Some admitted quite openly that they lived for fighting, and didn't much care who they fought or where they had to do it. Others turned out to be settlers whose lands had been taken by the Mexicans, or townsfolk who had seen their wooden homes go up in smoke as raiding Comanches had ridden suddenly out of the night to pillage and burn.

Several of the men claimed buffalo hunting as their livelihood. With the Mexican troubles coming to Texas these men of the prairie found their market for robes and meat fast disappearing and had drifted to the Alamo to find food and clothes at the expense of the Government.

Others, like Davy, had volunteered for different reasons. They valued independence above all else. Their spirit was the real spirit of America and of the Frontier in particular. They didn't parade their patriotism—in fact they were shy of speaking of it at all. They just felt deep down inside that if a land, a country, or an ideal was worth having, it was worth fighting for. These were the men of real grit—and there were many of them.

"Makes you feel kinda proud to be here," said Jake as they returned to the barracks. Davy had seldom heard the old hunter so serious. He felt moved himself, but in a different way. He felt the blood coursing through his veins with a sense of exhilaration. All his life he had fought for what he considered right, but it had been a lonely battle. In Congress, or in the Tennessee Legislature, his had seemed but one small voice crying out against injustice or wrong thinking. But to-night, on the battlements of the Alamo, he had unearthed the simple faith of ordinary men who thought much as he did. He was alone no more.

"Make sure you're right—then go ahead!" He spoke his motto out loud, with pride in his voice.

"You're durned right!" said Jake.

CHAPTER XXII

Santa Anna Arrives

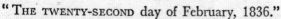

"The twenty-second day of February, 1836."

Davy wrote the date at the head of a blank page and settled down to make the latest entry in his diary. The quill felt awkward in his big hand, but he mastered the impulse to cast the book aside, and bent to his task. The candle threw long shadows on the walls as he wrote perched on his bunk beside the oaken table in the barrack-room. Around him lay the sleeping forms of his companions, contented snores sighing through the room to break the empty stillness of the night.

"Soon be time to go on duty," Davy thought, glancing at the window and seeing the first faint light of dawn encroaching on the pitch-black sky. He yawned lazily and stretched like a cat to ease his cramped muscles. He cocked an ear to the steady pacing of the sentries outside on the battlements, and heard the stamping of one man's feet as he tried to warm himself. Then suddenly, he heard a startled exclamation, a series of shouts, and the sound of running feet.

Davy jumped up, making for the door. As he reached

it, it was flung open and the bee-hunter burst into the room.

"He's arrived, Colonel!" he shouted, excitedly.

"Who's arrived?"

"Santa Anna!"

Davy whistled. "Now we'll see some action, lad," he grinned. "I was gettin' mighty tired o' waitin'."

They ran to the top parapet and strained their eyes into the half light towards the township.

"Over there," directed the bee-hunter, pointing to the river bank. The flames of a fire licked hungrily at the darkness, lighting up the white walls of the adobe buildings. Dark shapes could be seen moving busily in the shadows, like fidgeting ants. A tent sprang up as though by magic as they watched, and then another, and as the first light of morning flooded into the town a host of men and horses were disclosed in all directions.

"What do you see, Davy?" asked a quiet voice behind them as Colonel Bowie stepped up on to the parapet, rubbing the sleep from his eyes.

"Must be a thousand men at least, Colonel. Another half hour will tell us the worst."

Colonel Travis ran to join them, and soon the walls and parapets of the fortress were lined with curious figures, gazing at the Mexicans as they made camp and tended their horses. Their numbers seemed without end, for as soon as one company settled in another marched through the streets to join them. Farther to the south a column of foot soldiers wound down the trail to Bexar, and to the east a squadron of cavalry dismounted and turned their horses out to graze on a well-watered pasture.

By noon the whole of the Mexican army had arrived

in Bexar. Estimates of their strength varied, but all were agreed that at least seventeen hundred men were preparing to attack the Alamo. All that remained to be seen was whether Santa Anna intended to move against Goliad first.

Davy and his friends didn't have long to wait for the answer. Around two o'clock in the afternoon a lone rider came from the Mexican lines, and rode in the direction of the Fortress. The green and gold of his uniform was set off by two huge epaulettes, and topped by a tall, cockaded shako. He bore a white flag tied to the blade of his sword.

The Texans watched his progress towards them in silence. Colonel Bowie stepped out on to the flat top of the wall, arms folded across his chest, and feet wide apart. The Mexican cavalry officer halted when he was twenty yards from the Fort. He looked up at Bowie and shouted to him in excellent English.

"I weesh to speak with the Señor Bowie," he announced arrogantly.

"*Colonel* Bowie to you, my lad!" roared the commander, bristling at the Mexican's tone. The envoy shrugged as though the correction was of no moment. "Where is thees *Colonel* Bowie?" he asked. "Bring heem to me."

Bowie's face turned nearly purple as he strove to hold his temper. "*I* am Colonel Bowie," he cried. "Say your piece an' go before I come down there an' teach you how to speak to your betters."

"I am sorry, Colonel," the Mexican apologised with mock politeness. He bowed in exaggerated fashion from the waist. "I did not know. In our Army the officers dress like gentlemen."

"An' fight like yellow cowards!" Davy broke in, unable to contain himself any longer.

The Mexican ignored the remark and continued. "His Excellency General Santa Anna orders you to surrender at once to avoid bloodshed. Should you resist the Alamo weel be taken, and you weel be put to the sword. I await your answer."

"Then you can have it, by heaven!" roared Bowie. He turned and gave an order to one of his men. The fellow grinned and made for the corner of the central parapet where a large, black cannon was mounted on a wheeled carriage.

A minute later the elevated muzzle belched flame and smoke with a mighty roar of exploding gunpowder. A stirring cheer broke from the defenders as the ball flew through the air to smash into a house wall close to the first of the Mexican tents.

"That's my answer to His Excellency," Bowie told the officer scathingly. "Now get back before I lose my temper."

The horseman wheeled his mount without another word and galloped back to Bexar. The siege of the Alamo had commenced.

The first attack came at once. Five companies of foot soldiers formed up and marched to the limit of accurate rifle range. There they spread out to form an extended line and awaited the order to advance. Bowie strolled round the battlements completely unconcerned. He checked the positions of his men and spoke quietly and reassuringly to the younger, inexperienced fighters.

".Relax, lads," he told them. "Hold your fire until they're well in range, then make every shot tell. Don't let that pack o' jail-birds worry you. Keep calm an' watch the greasers run."

As he spoke a bugle shrilled from the Mexican ranks and the attack was on. The line of men moved forward at the double, urged on by their officers and the continuous blare of bugles. Half-way to the Alamo they halted and fired a ragged volley at the Texans. Then, reloading hastily, they streamed forward once more.

"What a way to fight!" said Jake, shaking his head sadly. "These greasers must want to die. Seems a shame to shoot 'em."

"Just a little longer!" yelled Bowie. "Pick your targets an' fire when I give the word." He waited until the Mexicans paused to fire again, then shouted his order abruptly.

The volley blasted forth from every window and wall in the Alamo. The Mexicans dropped by the score, their ranks shattered by the deadly accuracy of the bullets. The survivors stood dazed for precious seconds, and as they dived for cover among the rocks or behind the bodies of their comrades, a second volley tore into them. Despite the threats and exhortations of their officers they turned and ran.

Even then they found no safety, for Bowie had held his best marksmen in reserve, Davy and the bee-hunter among them. They leaned their rifles against the firmness of the window ledges where they stood and picked off the stragglers with calm deliberation. Man after man fell to their shots until the range became too great, and they were forced to hold their fire.

"That'll give *His Excellency* somethin' to think about," chortled Bowie, delighted with the deadly shooting of his men. "We won't have much more trouble today if I'm any judge."

Colonel Travis agreed. "They'll choose the darkness next time," he prophesied. "We'd better stand some of the men down to rest till nightfall."

"There's sense in that," Bowie agreed. He detailed Davy and his company to withdraw to the barracks and then settled down to the long wait until the next attack began.

But no alarum broke the peace of the night. Sentries were changed at regular intervals, and all reported no sign of activity from the Mexican lines. It looked as though Santa Anna was too busy licking his wounds to risk another attack.

Daylight brought no change. The Americans could see their enemies drilling and parading among their tents and piles of equipment. They saw Santa Anna himself ride through the lines inspecting, and gesticulating to his officers to emphasise some point of military procedure. It was as though the Mexicans had decided to ignore the presence of the Alamo and its little garrison.

Davy was puzzled. "I don't like it, Jake," he said to the old hunter with a frown. "There's somethin' up."

"What?"

"Wish I knew. But of one thing I'm sure. Santa Anna ain't the kind o' man to take a lickin' an' not take his revenge for it. He's got somethin' up his sleeve all right."

"Perhaps he's decided to attack Goliad first, after all."

"Maybe," Davy replied, doubtfully. "But I think there's more to it than that."

"Colonel Bowie seems quite happy," said Jake, " an' so's Travis. They're both stalking about like dogs with two tails, tickled to death with the pastin' we gave the Mex's yesterday."

Davy smiled. "Friend Bowie would be happy whatever happened. He's a real fine feller. But all the same I still think we're in for a surprise—an' not a very pleasant one at that."

CHAPTER XXIII

Mission to Goliad

"Boom!"

The sound of the explosion woke Davy with a start next morning. He lay in his blankets for a few seconds to collect his wits, and then hurried to the window. A second explosion greeted him from the direction of the river, and next instant he heard a crash of masonry from inside the Fort.

Santa Anna's secret was out. An artillery battery was installed among the willows, some three hundred and fifty yards from the Fortress.

All day long the barrage continued with monotonous regularity. First solid ball was fired, then grape shot, until the defenders' nerves were frayed and their heads ached from the noise. The damage caused was not sufficient to worry about, but lack of sleep turned cheerful men into quick-tempered, irritable creatures, as the strain began to tell.

"We *must* get word to Goliad and Gonzales," said

Travis, as he, Bowie and Davy sat discussing the situation after two days of bombardment.

"I'll go," Davy offered, but his companions wouldn't hear of it.

"You're far too valuable here," Bowie told him. "We can't spare you. It means callin' for a volunteer—but he'll have to be a wily bird who can slip through the enemy lines, *and* get back again with news."

"That means an older man, an' one of our best horses," said Davy thoughtfully. "A man on foot would get through easily enough, but his chances of stealin' a horse to take him to Goliad are pretty slim. The only way is to leave in the early hours, when the Mexican sentries are slackest, an' trust to speed to carry him through."

"I think you're probably right," agreed Travis, and Bowie nodded his consent.

"Got any suggestions, Davy?"

"All o' my men will volunteer. The trouble will be holding 'em back. They're fresher than your boys, so it's only fair that one o' them should go. Let's put it to them."

Davy and the two officers made for the barrack-room and put their request to the men. Without hesitation the entire company stepped forward, eager to undertake the perilous mission. They argued among themselves heatedly as they asserted their right to be chosen. Jake and Thimblerig nearly came to blows, and the bee-hunter's voice rose high above the babble of conversation as he pleaded with Davy to let him go.

"Quiet!" roared their leader in feigned anger. "You

fellers sound like a gaggle o' geese in a cornfield. You'd better leave it to me to pick one o' you—then there won't be any more bickerin' an' actin' like a pack o' kids."

They stood silently as Davy walked up and down their ranks, considering each man in turn. Every eye was on his tall figure, and he began to wonder if the choice he had in the back of his mind was right after all. He hesitated briefly, then, brushing aside his doubts, he stopped in front of one of his men.

"Pirate," he announced, "you're the man for me, if you're still willin' to go."

"The saints be praised, Colonel!" cried the sailor, his eyes twinkling with pleasure. "'Tis me own self that will bless you for your choice, an' delighted I'll be to show these landlubbers how to sail through shark-infested waters!"

"Not so much o' your blarney, pirate," Davy grinned, "or I might change my mind. Slip down to the stables an' pick the best o' the Mexican horses we brought in. Then report to Colonel Bowie—an' good luck to you."

The pirate scuttled off as though fearful that Davy would reverse his decision. His bearded face was wreathed in smiles, and he laughed uproariously at his good fortune as he heard the dismayed howls of his companions.

"That's a fine thing!" exclaimed Jake bitterly. "Fancy choosing that old rogue instead o' me!"

"The pot calling the kettle black," said Thimblerig with a smile, and he had to duck sharply to avoid the old hunter's swinging fist.

Davy stepped between the two men and caught hold of their arms.

" Save your fightin' for Santa Anna," he warned them severely. " All you men are forgettin' one thing, an' that's the most important point of all."

" What's that, Davy?" came a chorus of voices.

" Why, the pirate's the only man jack among you who speaks the Mexican lingo! He can bluff his way through the sentries in the darkness if he has to."

The pirate chose a spell when the moon was hidden by a thick black cloud to make his exit from the Alamo.

Colonel Bowie and Davy let him out through the partly opened main gate, whispered their good-lucks and watched as the shadows of the great walls swallowed up horse and rider. They waited for several minutes, but no sound came to their ears. The pirate was taking no chance of being discovered as he threaded his way between the Mexican sentries.

" Looks as though he's goin' to make it," whispered Davy as the minutes mounted and still no breath of sound disturbed the silence.

" Let's hope so," answered Bowie's voice from beside him. His tone was so dejected and weary that Davy looked round in surprise. The commander's face shone deathly white in the eerie half light, and he thought he saw a shiver pass over the man's body.

" Is anythin' the matter, Colonel?" he asked anxiously.

" I don't quite know, Davy. I've been feelin' queer all day. It's nothin'. It'll probably pass off in a while. I . . . I . . ."

Colonel Bowie's next words were inaudible. He slumped forward and fell to the ground before Davy could reach out to catch him. He was unconscious by the time they had carried him to his quarters.

*   *   *

Barrett Travis straightened up from bending over the sleeping form of his fellow colonel. His brow was ridged with worry, and his tired eyes lacked lustre. He passed a hand over his face in a gesture of utter helplessness.

" He's a very sick man, Davy." He spoke in a whisper, as though half afraid that the words would penetrate the merciful oblivion that shrouded Bowie's mind.

Davy nodded sadly. " Must've worked himself to a standstill," he muttered.

" He's had no proper rest for weeks. I couldn't get him to ease up at all. Even when he was off duty he would sit and plan or worry about what was happening at Goliad, or what luck Houston was having with the raising of an army. I don't know what we'll do without him."

" One thing's certain, anyway," said Davy firmly. " You will have to take command from now on, Colonel. I'll back you to the utmost—but it's your command, an' it couldn't be in better hands."

Travis didn't waste time protesting. He knew there was no point in arguing with Davy when his tone was as definite as that. He straightened the blankets on the bed and then led the way from the room. Without a word Davy followed and joined the new commander outside in the cool night air. Wordlessly the two men matched their paces and walked across the courtyard and up the steps to the battlements. They strolled up and down between the sentries for a while, deep in thought. At length Travis broke the silence.

"What do you think of our chances, Davy?" he asked at length.

Davy paused before answering. He studied the intense expression on the young Colonel's face and read the courage in his eyes.

"Do you want an honest answer?" he inquired.

"Of course."

"Then here it is. If reinforcements don't arrive within a week we ain't got a chance in a million o' holdin' out. You know that as well as I do. But I'll tell you one thing," he added, "there'll be no surrender, an' Santa Anna will pay dear if he does get into the Alamo."

Travis nodded. "That's about the size of it," he agreed. "But I wish we could do something about that artillery. It hasn't caused a single casualty in two days, but it doesn't give us an hour's peace all day. If it goes on much longer our nerves'll be all to pieces."

"I know," said Davy, "an' I've been figurin' it's about time we hit back at those Mexican gunners. Leave it to me. I'll see what can be done in the mornin'."

CHAPTER XXIV

Long Betsy talks to Santa Anna

———————/⟨≈≈⟩/———————

Davy stood at the window and watched the shadows underneath the willows for the first sign of movement. Behind him Jake Marshall loaded six rifles in succession and laid them carefully on the table that was drawn up to the wall.

"Won't be long now, Jake. Three o' the varmints are walkin' up from the tents. Give me Long Betsy so's I can give them a welcome in a minute."

Jake handed the rifle to his friend and waited for further orders. He saw Davy raise the weapon to his shoulder and peered over his friend's back to watch. He saw the first of the Mexican gunners reach the ugly black cannon and ram home a charge. The second man fed the grape-shot down the muzzle, while the third stood ready with a lighted taper.

Davy waited for the moment when the flame was moving out towards the touch hole. He caught the man's chest in the direct line of his front and back sights, and pressed the trigger. Long Betsy spoke with a vicious bark, and the gunner twisted backwards to fall at the feet of his startled companions.

The first man snatched up the taper and thrust it forward again, but he was too late, for Davy had grabbed a second rifle from Jake's eager hands and fired in the twinkling of an eye. The Mexican fell across the body of his fellow.

The third gunner tried to fire the cannon, only to meet the same fate, and Jake began to chuckle with glee. "Like playin' skittles!" he grinned.

"There's another gun team comin' up," Davy warned him. "Get those rifles loaded again. I may be needin' them in a hurry."

Two more gunners fell to Davy's sharp-shooting before the Mexicans abandoned all hope of firing the cannon. They retreated out of range to join their fellows at the other guns of the battery.

Davy spent most of the morning at the window, picking off any man who grew too venturesome, but he could do no more than silence one gun of the battery. The others kept up a continuous bombardment of the Alamo, causing more damage than the defenders liked to see.

The casualties among the men of the Fort began to mount, for it was grape-shot entirely that was being poured in now. The Mexicans had forsaken solid ball completely. Thimblerig was the first to be struck. The scattering shot ricocheted from the inner walls and caught him a glancing blow in the chest. He lay groaning on the packed earth of the courtyard, fighting for breath, his ribs feeling as though they had been kicked by a fiery Spanish mule.

The bee-hunter rushed to his aid—careless of the bullets that whistled all around him from the rifles of Mexican snipers. Davy saw him stagger as he reached the top of the steps leading down to the courtyard, but he regained his balance and ran to the fallen gambler.

"I'll be all right, lad," said Thimblerig a few moments later as he lay cradled in the bee-hunter's arms. "Don't think there's any real damage. Just bruised me an' nearly knocked the stuffin' out!"

The bee-hunter helped him to his feet and led him to the shade. He sat the gambler down on a bench and took a seat beside him.

"Nearly caught one myself, Thimbles," he remarked casually. He pointed to a gaping rent in the breast of his jacket, and began undoing his shirt buttons with a shaking hand.

"How on earth did you survive that one?" exclaimed the gambler. "Why man, it's not an inch away from your heart!"

The bee-hunter didn't reply. Instead he fished inside his shirt, and drew out a battered leather-bound book. Thimblerig saw a jagged gash in the front cover, and the whiteness of torn pages. In the centre of the gash lay a leaden bullet. He glanced at the title as the book was held out for him to see. Carefully worked in gold leaf the inscription read *The Holy Bible*.

"I've never been without it since I left home," the bee-hunter told him simply.

But their wonder at the miraculous escape was rudely interrupted by a cry from the battlements. They looked up and saw one of the sentries pointing excitedly towards the east. Colonel Travis and Davy ran to join him, and next moment the alarm was ringing through the Fort. Santa Anna was mounting another big attack.

The rest of the day seemed one continual battle. The

main attack was beaten off as before, but Santa Anna was not to be discouraged so easily. He sent in skirmishing parties from all directions at once. Small, fast-mounted groups of cavalry sped towards the Alamo, fired once at the loopholes, and raced back to their own lines on a zig-zag course. The snipers redoubled their efforts at the same time, and foot soldiers worked their way from cover to cover while the defenders were distracted by the horsemen. And all the time the cannon boomed their venom from the river bank.

Colonel Travis was everywhere. Pale and tired though he was, he never relaxed all day, stirring the men to a further fury of activity when they began to flag, tending the wounded, or helping to bring up fresh supplies of water, food or ammunition. He was an inspiration to them all.

Davy and Jake were kept busy at their vantage point high up in the wall of the main building. They fired and re-loaded alternately, until their rifles grew almost too hot to hold. For a while the Mexican snipers concentrated their fire on the open window, forcing the two marksmen to find a safer spot, and before long they found themselves driven from first one window and then another by the relentless bullets.

"Worn a hole in my moccasins already," grumbled Jake as he gazed ruefully at the sole of his right foot.

"That'll get some fat off for you," Davy laughed. "Haven't seen you do so much runnin' about in years."

"Quite like old times," said the grizzled hunter later as they sat on the floor during a lull and chewed laboriously at sandwiches of stale bread and dried jerky. "Only one thing missin' though."

"What's that, Jake?"

"Young George Russell an' Luke Peters. They were good lads to be in a spot o' trouble with."

Davy nodded. "What did happen to George?" he asked. "I lost touch with him when I went to Washington. Ain't heard a word about him from that day on."

"The last I heard was that he was headin' West with a party o' settlers, but quite where to I don't recollect."

Another burst of firing and the sound of galloping hooves brought the two men to their feet abruptly. They got into action just in time to break up a sortie from an unexpected quarter, dropping the bearded officer who led the Mexicans, and severely wounding three of his men.

"That was a near one!" Davy exclaimed as the cavalry retreated, and he paused to wipe the perspiration from his brow. "Wonder how it was the boys on this section o' the wall didn't stop them?"

"Better take a look," Jake muttered, making for the door.

He found what he had feared. A dying volunteer leaned against the parapet in a pool of blood, and around him lay the huddled forms of three more men. Jake hurried across and knelt beside the first man. Trembling eyelids opened briefly as he tried to speak.

"What was that, son?" asked the hunter gently.

"Snipers. There." The dying man tried desperately to lift his arm and point, and as Jake turned a bullet screamed over his head to flatten itself against the wall.

"Watch out, Davy!" he yelled, flinging himself flat. "Don't step out for a minute." He crawled to the far end of the battlement and peered through a loophole in the

direction from which the shot had come. He couldn't
see anything at first, but presently a movement and the
glint of metal caught his eye, high up in one of the swaying willow trees. A sniper was sitting with his feet astride
a thick limb, waiting for another easy target.

"I'll settle you, my beauty," Jake growled angrily. He
crawled back into the room from which he had come, and
went to join Davy.

"Bit o' pigeon shootin' for you," he said, indicating
the treetop with a gnarled finger.

"Just my mark," Davy grinned. "How that greaser
got up there without us seein' beats me."

Long Betsy made short work of the unsuspecting sniper.
Amid a flurry of falling leaves he tumbled from his perch
and hit the ground twenty feet below with a thud that
could be heard right inside the room. He moved no more,
his broken rifle laying beside him in the sand of the river
bank.

The two men resumed their interrupted meal. The
dry food took a lot of swallowing, and presently Davy
ambled off to fetch a billy can of water to help wash it
down. To his surprise he found a guard mounted by the
water tanks that held the whole supply for the Alamo.

"What's up?" he asked.

"Colonel Travis told me not to let anyone have water
without his permission," the volunteer told him.

"Why?"

"He didn't say, but he looked mighty worried."

Davy was puzzled at the order. He went in search of
the commander and found him in Colonel Bowie's quarters. Bowie was a little better, but he was still a very
sick man. He tried to smile as he saw Davy's tall figure

appear in the doorway, but it was obviously a great effort, and he sank back on the pillows without managing more than a flicker of pleasure at the sight of his friend.

"What's all this about no water being taken?" Davy asked Travis quietly. "Are we runnin' short?"

"Worse than that Davy," Travis told him. "Santa Anna's men are trying to cut off the supply. It comes from a pipeline out of a spring by the river. He's only just realised where it is, so I'm getting all the tanks as full as I can before he stops the flow."

"Sounds serious," said Davy grimly.

"It is. We can't hold more than enough for a week or so, at most, but there's nothing we can do about it."

"How far away is the spring?"

"Well within rifle range. But the Mexicans are working at night to block the pipes, and we can't keep them off."

"We'll have to see about that," said Davy. He turned to Bowie. "D'you mind if I borrow your knife, Colonel?" he asked.

"Help yourself," the sick Colonel told him. "I shan't be needin' it."

Davy picked up the dreadful weapon and strapped it to his belt. "Thanks," he said briefly. "I'll see you get it back some time to-night."

"What have you got in mind Davy?" Travis inquired. "I'm getting to know you by now. When that gleam comes into your eyes it means trouble for someone."

"Just a little rib-tickling, with your permission, Colonel," Davy told him with a smile. "I aim to take a short stroll to-night in the moonlight. Any objections?"

"None whatever. But be careful."

"I'm always careful," said Davy. "Too durned scared half the time to be anythin' else!"

*   *   *

Three shadowy figures dropped from a rope that dangled down the rear wall of the Alamo. Their faces blacked and the backs of their hands covered by thin gloves, they merged with the darkness and disappeared from sight.

"Not a word out o' you till we get back, or I'll skin you alive," Davy whispered to Thimblerig as they crept forward into the night. The gambler laughed silently, his white teeth flashing in the darkness. Beside him Jake Marshall felt his way cautiously forward with the craft and cunning of his long years of experience in the woods of Tennessee.

They took their time, and didn't reach the spring for the best part of half an hour. They heard the hushed voices of the Mexican sentries as they met on their rounds. They listened to the stirring and stamping of hobbled horses in the cavalry lines, and picked out the occasional snores of sleeping soldiers in the tents farther back on the edge of Bexar. They lay in the depth of a thick bed of rushes and watched the Mexicans as they bent in the water to ram rocks and clay into the mouth of the water pipe.

Four men worked in the detail at the spring. There was no room for more. One brought up the materials on the back of a mule; another handed them to a man who stood in the middle of the spring; while two more attended to the blocking operation.

"We'll take the mule man first," Davy whispered to his friends. "Thimbles, you catch the mule while I deal with the Mex. Jake stands by in case of trouble."

They nodded to show they understood and together the three men crept forward into the open.

The mule driver never knew what hit him. The naked steel of Bowie's knife flashed once in the pale moonlight before it sank into his body. Davy's hand stifled any groans that might have escaped to warn the others. He rolled the body to one side and stepped forward, taking the mule's lead rope from Thimblerig's hand. He stopped short of the spring and clicked his fingers to attract the second Mexican's attention. The man looked up to see an indistinct form beckoning him to come out of the water. Grumbling softly to himself the Mexican stepped up on to the bank, thinking Davy was his friend.

A blow from Thimblerig felled him in his tracks, and it took but a few minutes longer to tackle the two remaining soldiers. Ten minutes' work freed the water pipes completely, and the three Americans crept back to the Fort, well pleased with their outing.

"That'll give Travis a chance to fill every container we've got in the Alamo," Davy chuckled later, when they were back in the safety of the barrack-room. "No doubt the Mexicans will have another go to-morrow night, with guards to stop us interferin', but at least we've gained a day's supply."

"Reckon we can have that drink now," said Jake, reaching for the billy-can.

CHAPTER XXV

The Pirate Returns

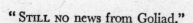

" STILL NO news from Goliad."

Colonel Travis sank wearily to a sitting position on the courtyard steps beside Davy. His eyes were red-rimmed from lack of sleep and the smoke of gunpowder, and his body shook from the fever that racked his flesh.

" No news is good news," Davy answered cheerfully. " The pirate will get through if it's humanly possible— after all, he's only been gone a few days."

Travis sighed deeply and closed his eyes to try and snatch a brief respite from his duties. Both men were heedless of the bullets that sliced the air above their heads, or the boom of the artillery battery. A handful of volunteers kept up a desultory fire at the Mexicans, while others sat and nursed their wounds or lay sleeping like exhausted hounds in odd corners of the buildings.

A heavy depression seemed to fill the air, sapping the vitality of the men and making them listless and dejected. Yet still the Alamo held out against the hordes of Mexicans surrounding its walls. Still the Americans rose to meet each new threat, and sent the enemy fleeing headlong in retreat. How they did it no one quite knew, least of all the volunteers themselves. Under a hundred men of the original garrison remained—and half of them were wounded in some degree.

Water was now strictly rationed and food running short. The defenders had been forced to slaughter some of their horses to provide fresh meat, and the sickness, that had struck at Colonel Bowie, was even now reducing Colonel Travis to a caricature of his former energetic self.

The first of March had come and gone without a let-up in the relentless pressure of General Santa Anna and his troops. The second, third, and fourth days of the month had followed with monotonous sameness, until all sense of date and time seemed lost. Daylight and dark, attack and counter-attack—these were the only things that came with unfailing regularity, and with the dawn of the fifth of March the pattern showed no sign of change.

Even Thimblerig was silent now, his tongue as still as the forgotten thimbles in his waistcoat pocket. The bee-hunter sang softly to himself of lands across the seas, or mournful ditties of lost causes and battles of long ago. Jake Marshall's friendly grumbles and growling speech were seldom heard. He reserved all his energies for picking off the Mexicans with silent concentration—broken only by his angry mutter as a shot went wide, or an enemy bullet sang too close for comfort.

Davy alone maintained some measure of cheerfulness. The perpetual grin that so many men had known and grown to love in hard times and in peaceful days, was a trifle strained—but it was still to be seen lurking in the humorous lines of his mouth, and in the laughter creases at the corners of his eyes. The sprightliness of his step was gone, but he still managed to hold himself with pride and was ever ready to lend a hand where it was most needed. He had found an old guitar among the relics of better days in the storerooms of the Alamo, and in the cool of the evening he strummed away, composing tuneless songs of defiance to Mexico, and rude ditties about Santa Anna.

It was late afternoon on this fifth day of March when the sentry on the northern wall brought them all to their feet with his shrill cry.

"What's up, lad?" called Davy as he sprang to his post.

"Two riders on the skyline, Davy. They're headed this way—an' it looks as though half the Mex cavalry is after them."

"It's the pirate!" Davy exclaimed a few moments later as his eyes picked out the bearded face of the first horseman. He didn't recognise the second man, and yet there was something familiar about the way he rode, urging his horse to greater efforts.

Everyone crowded to the parapet to watch the life and death chase that was being run through the chaparral of the sandy wastes to the north. Slowly the two horsemen increased their lead on the Mexicans, until it seemed almost certain that they would reach the safety of the Fort in time. Then, with piercing clarity, the cry of another sentry filled their hearts with dismay.

"Look! There's another squadron leavin' Bexar to head them off!"

Davy took in the situation at a glance. He whirled about to face Colonel Travis. "We *must* save those men!" he cried. "With your permission, Colonel, I'll lead a sortie to their aid."

Travis rose to the occasion with the swiftness of a born commander. "Of course," he uttered briefly. "We'll give you covering fire and be ready on the gate to let you in when you return."

Davy only waited to hear his first words before he was running at the double to the stables with Jake and Thimblerig and the bee-hunter close behind. They grabbed saddles from pegs on the walls and flung them across the backs of the first horses they reached. A quick pull on the girth, a twist of the stirrup leathers, hastily buckled bridles and they were away, clattering across the courtyard and out of the barely-open gate.

At a mad gallop they tore off across the muddy turf to meet the pirate and his hard-pressed companion. Snipers' bullets followed them, but they travelled too fast for accurate shooting. They rode as they had never ridden before—straight for the oncoming cavalry.

The watchers on the battlements saw them reach the pirate and wave him on towards the Fort. But even as the bearded sailor slowed to speak to Davy he fell across the neck of his horse—the victim of a shot from the fast-approaching Mexicans. His companion swerved his horse to come alongside and helped the wounded man regain control of his mount while Davy and his three friends reined hard and fired a volley at the Mexicans.

The leading cavalryman tumbled headlong from his horse to join two more of his countrymen beneath the thrashing hooves of the galloping horses. The riders tried desperately to swerve away from their bodies, but they were too close. Two horses tripped and fell, throwing their riders clear over the necks to land head first in the mud.

The pirate, helped by his companion, was now well out of danger and nearly at the open gate of the Alamo. Davy and his friends stayed where they were for precious minutes while they re-loaded and fired once more. Then they wheeled their horses and raced back in the wake of the others.

The second troop of Mexicans were now too close for comfort, and as the Americans' horses gathered speed the puff of exploding gunpowder came from their rifles. The bee-hunter was seen to jerk upright, clutching at his back. He collapsed in the saddle, but stayed there, sprawled head forward, held on the terrified animal's back by the locking of his feet in the stirrups and the grip of his fingers in the horse's mane.

A withering burst of shots broke out from the Fort as Colonel Travis directed the covering fire, and without a pause the four horses pounded through the gates and into the courtyard. The great doors slammed shut behind them as the thwarted Mexicans rode past, swerving this way and that to avoid the bullets.

Someone seized the bridle of the bee-hunter's horse, and held it fast while eager hands reached up to disentangle his feet from the stirrup irons, and bring him gently to the ground. But the lad was past the aid of man. He died in Thimblerig's arms without speaking once.

The pirate was luckier. His wound was in the fleshy part of his shoulder, and, although shock and loss of blood had drained the colour from his face, he raised enough strength to climb out of the saddle and join his friends. The man who had journeyed with him stepped forward to take his weight on a sturdy arm, and help him to a bench beside the wall of the barracks. It was then that Jake let out a cry of surprise.

"Great sufferin' snakes! Look who's here, Davy!"

Davy looked up from beside the bee-hunter. He glanced in the direction of the stranger, but his back was turned and he couldn't see his face. Something stirred in his memory as he gazed at the line of the man's broad shoulders and narrow hips—but it was elusive. He felt sure he had met the man somewhere before, but quite when or where he couldn't tell.

Then, suddenly and without warning, the stranger turned.

It was George Russell! "Hello Davy," he smiled, striding to meet the man who had taught him all he knew of bear hunting and scouting for the Army.

"By all that's wonderful!" Davy exclaimed. "Never thought to see you in these parts, George." He grinned from ear to ear with the pleasure of the meeting. "What in blazes are you doin' in Texas?" he asked.

"Might as well ask you the same thing," the younger man grinned. "The pirate told me you an' Jake were at the Alamo—so here I am. Couldn't trust you two on your own any longer. There's no knowin' what mischief you'd get up to."

"Cheeky young pup!" growled the voice of Jake, his gruffness belying the affection in his eyes.

George Russell punched the old hunter playfully on the chest. "Not so much o' the *young*, Jake," he cried. "It's a tidy spell since we fought together at the Coosa an' Ten Islands."

"Too true, lad," Jake agreed, pushing his hat over

one eye as he scratched the silver hairs of his head. " But it's mighty good to see you, none the less."

Davy linked his arms through those of his two old friends and led them off to where the pirate reported to Colonel Travis, while his wound was being dressed. " Nothin' like hearin' bad news in good company," he smiled.

CHAPTER XXVI

Colonel Travis draws The Line

————◦◦◦◦————

THE PIRATE'S news was even worse than they had expected.

"There's not a hope o' gettin' a single man to join us," he told them bluntly. "These Mexicans are as numerous as seagulls round a fishin' boat. They're swarmin' up from Mexico City in shoals."

"You mean to say there's more soldiers on the way?" Travis asked incredulously. "Why man, there's close on two thousand in Bexar as it is!"

The pirate shook his head sadly. "Sure an' 'tis the truth I'm tellin' you, Colonel," he sighed. "If you don't believe me ask young George here."

"He's right," George stated in agreement. "We were settin' out from Goliad to join you when five hundred o' the Mex cavalry drove our force back into the town. The pirate an' I had to slip out at night to bring you news."

"An' that ain't all," went on the sailor. "We saw another five hundred ridin' to join the first force. I reckon Santa Anna's got four thousand men at his command."

Davy sighed. "An' here were we, thinkin' Goliad was safe because no troops left Bexar to attack it!"

By now all the men in the Alamo, with the exception of the sentries, had gathered round their commander. They squatted on the ground, Indian fashion, or leaned against the walls as they listened to the talk. Some rested on the benches or on the steps; others stood silently with their hands clasped about the muzzles of their weapons. The setting sun cast a red glow on the hollows of their grimed cheeks and unshaven chins, while the light breeze of evening ruffled the matted locks of their hair.

Their eyes were expressionless, their thoughts private. They knew what the pirate's news meant to the future of the Alamo. They knew without being told that there was in fact *no* future for any of them. Even as they listened, they dreamt of the green woods and pastures of their native States, of the families they had left behind, and of the days of peace that seemed so long ago.

The hunters among them knew that they would never again hear the gobble of a wild turkey, or see the fall of a mighty buffalo on the wild, free prairie. The farmers thought sadly of the frolics of harvest time that they would join in no more, and of the wholesome, satisfying smell of fresh-ploughed furrows. Their faces were set and grim, but they hid their thoughts from each other, even as the cold chill of fear crept through them and turned their stomachs to water.

A strange silence descended on the Alamo as they looked into each other's eyes and waited for their commander to speak.

"What I have to say is for all to hear," Travis told them. He led the way into the barrack-room and stood in the centre of the long, low building—surrounded by the survivors of his garrison, and flanked by the cots and mattresses of the sick and dying. Davy saw Colonel Bowie raise himself on one elbow to catch what was to be said.

"You have all heard the news," Travis told them. "All hope of relief has gone. The Alamo is the gateway into Texas, and we alone are left to hold it. We can at best hold out for a few days more, and then the Alamo will fall. Of that there is no doubt. But I intend to fight the Mexicans until there is no breath left in my body. There will be no surrender—it will be a fight to the death."

The fever-ridden commander unsheathed his sword with a flourish and drew a line in the packed earth of the floor. "I give my full permission to any man to escape from the Fort as best he can before the final assault begins. You are all free to leave at once and chance getting through the Mexican lines alive. But all those who wish to stay and fight Santa Anna to the death must walk across this line. The choice is yours."

So saying Barrett Travis stepped back to the far end of the room and waited for the reaction of his men.

Davy strode to join him with a smile on his lips, and every man in the barrack-room followed suit. Colonel Bowie's voice came from the shadows of the room, pleading for someone to carry him across the line. "I'm not bein' left out at this stage in the game," he said, a wan smile playing round his mouth. Davy picked him up as gently as though he were a child and walked across the line with the former commander in his arms.

The defenders of the Alamo had made their decision. It was to be a fight to the death—with no quarter given or expected.

CHAPTER XXVII

The Final Assault

THE MORNING of 6th March dawned bright and clear. A sense of expectancy hung over the Alamo as the defenders lined the walls and stared towards Bexar and the Mexican lines.

Word had come to them during the night that Santa Anna was about to start an all-out attack on the Fortress with every man he had at his command. The roll of drums and the blare of bugles came to their ears as they waited, and they saw the swarthy, black-haired infantry-men form up in battle order before their tents. Frenzied activity was apparent in the cavalry lines. Horses stirred restlessly as they waited for the touch of the silver spurs that would send them hurtling forward to the attack. Men ran back and forth, buckling on their sword belts, or making last-minute adjustments to their equipment and the harness of their mounts.

Davy kept his eyes glued on the square marquee that housed Santa Anna and his staff. When the flap moved back and the gaudy, bemedalled figure of the over-dressed General stepped into sight, the battle would be on.

"I'd give my eyes to get that peacock in my sights," he muttered to Jake Marshall. "Just one crack at him an' I'd die happy."

"You might miss the target—like you did at Little Rock," said the old hunter with a sly grin.

"What d'you mean, Jake?" Davy was puzzled by his friend's words. "I didn't miss the target at that shootin' match. I won, didn't I?"

Jake chuckled happily. "Not by a mile, Davy. *I* won that match for you."

The light of understanding dawned in Davy's eyes. "Are you tryin' to tell me you rigged that target?" he asked.

"Of course I did," Jake told him. "You don't think I'd let that no-good Joshua feller get the laugh on Colonel Davy Crockett, do you? Somethin' must've been wrong with the powder that day, so I made sure the target told a different tale."

Davy roared with laughter. "You cheatin' old rogue!" he spluttered. "I *knew* there was somethin' queer about that second shot. How did you manage it?"

Jake smiled happily at the memory. "Just picked up a spent bullet when no one was lookin', an' stuck it in the hole," he told his friend casually, as though it were an everyday occurrence.

"I'll take you back to Little Rock one day an' see you're tarred an' feathered," Davy laughed. "What would've happened if you had been caught?"

"I'm never caught," said Jake modestly.

"Boom!"

The roar of the cannon blasted out from the willows, to be followed by a second and then a third, as the entire battery came to life and hurled the deadly grape-shot into the Fort. The bugles in Bexar shrilled out in a chorus, the drums reached a crescendo—and the attack was on.

The Mexicans flooded towards the Fort from all directions. Wave after wave of infantrymen poured out of the town. The cavalry raced ahead of them, drawing the fire of the defenders in an attempt to shield the foot soldiers. They fired as they rode, then wheeled and reloaded while circling to attack again.

Leaden bullets spattered against the wall of the parapet like hail. They ricocheted across the courtyard, and screamed viciously at the Americans from all sides. A curtain of smoke rose up to hide the advancing men, and the din grew more than human eardrums could stand. Colonel Travis sprang to the battlements to direct the fire of his men, but his words were lost in the fearful barrage of the cannon. They saw his lips moving but no sound reached their ears.

Volley after volley crashed forth from the walls, from Davy and the volunteers around him. They snatched up fresh rifles, while waiting men re-loaded rapidly behind them. They didn't need to aim as the tight-packed mass of green uniforms pressed ever onward through the smoke and dust that shrouded them. The first lines of Mexicans were cut to ribbons. They tried to break, but the relentless pressure of the men behind forced them forward. Behind their ranks the officers urged the yelling men to the attack at the points of their swords. They were taking no chances with the convict rabble that formed the spearhead of their attack. Men turned to run and were shot down by their own officers with cold deliberation.

On and on they came until they reached the walls of the Alamo. A battering ram appeared as though by magic, held high by twenty or thirty men. The great baulk of timber struck, and struck again at the iron-bound door of the Fort, as the defenders tried desperately to pick off the men who held it.

Davy saw Jake Marshall lean forward from the parapet to fire downwards at the Mexicans below him. As his head and shoulders left the protective cover of the wall a bullet struck the old man and he fell backwards, tumbling to the floor of the courtyard. Another volunteer sprang to take his place, only to fall to a second hail of bullets.

Davy looked about him quickly. Half the defenders were now dead or wounded. George Russell staggered beside him, a bullet wound in one arm.

" It's no good Davy!" he screamed above the noise. " That door will give in a minute. We must get back to the barracks!"

Davy nodded silently. He bent double and ran the length of the battlements, touching each survivor on the shoulder and pointing to the main building.

" Fall back to the barracks as fast as you can!" he yelled.

One by one the Americans left their posts and retreated down the steps, across the courtyard, and into the building. They passed the body of Colonel Travis where he lay before the main door, the victim of a stray shot. Even as the last men reached the barracks the battering ram broke through the door, splintering the great timber bar that held it fast. The cast-iron hinges snapped in half and the Mexicans appeared in the opening, fighting their way through the jagged wood that still barred their passage.

"Slam them!" Davy cried, raising Long Betsy to his shoulder and firing into the opening at point-blank range. But there was no holding the attackers. The door fell inwards with a crash that shook the very foundations of the Alamo, and the screaming hordes poured into the Fort.

Davy slammed the door of the barracks shut and eager hands thrust the great oaken table tight against it. Chairs, tables, packing-cases—all were piled against the door in a desperate attempt to hold it secure while a pitifully small number of men kept up a ragged fire from the windows.

"Get back against that wall!" Davy yelled. "Hold your fire for a last volley—then every man for himself."

No more than twenty men were left by now. They retreated to the far wall and waited wearily for the door to give way to the merciless battering it was receiving. Davy saw the wounded George Russell stagger up the small flight of steps behind them and make for the tiny door, high in the wall.

"Where are you off to?" he cried.

"The powder magazine," George shouted back. He reached for a candle that burned in a bracket holder on the wall, and threw open the door to the magazine.

"Hold it until the greasers break in!" Davy roared. "We'll take as many o' them with us as we can."

With a sickening crunch the barrack-room door collapsed. The furniture piled against it rocked and fell, and the first Mexicans broke in.

"Fire!" Davy shouted, and every rifle spoke defiantly.

But more men pushed forward, and there was no time to re-load. The dying Colonel Bowie lifted up two horse pistols from the blankets of his bed and fired blindly in one last gesture of defiance.

Davy saw George Russell fall to a Mexican bullet. The candle rolled to the ground, miraculously staying alight. Thimblerig jumped to retrieve it and flung himself up the steps. Even as his hand reached forward to explode the gunpowder a bullet caught him. He hung motionless on the top step for a brief moment, then fell to the floor at Davy's feet. The three silver thimbles spilled from his waistcoat pocket and lay still on the barrack-room floor. The gambler had played his last game.

Davy whirled Long Betsy high above his head, striking at the swords and bayonets that ringed him. He felt the beautiful walnut of the stock shatter as he struck and struck again, and a blinding wave of anger passed through him. He threw the useless rifle at the faces of the Mexicans and drew his hunting knife from its sheath. He lunged and parried and thrust, fighting as he had never fought before. A bullet struck his head, burning its way across his brow. He faltered momentarily then fell to his knees, and knew no more.

*   *   *

Colonel Davy Crockett lay unconscious, wounded by the Mexicans, after fighting in a strange land to protect settlers he had never met. Faithful to his ideals, loyal to his country, and true to his motto—" Make sure you're right, then go ahead "—Davy Crockett had fought on, even against impossible odds.